IMAGES
of America

JEWISH
SOUTH JERSEY

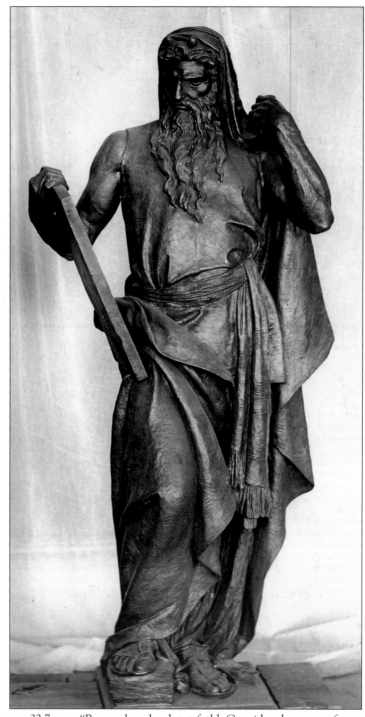

As Deuteronomy 32:7 says, "Remember the days of old. Consider the years of ages past."

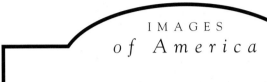

IMAGES
of America

JEWISH
SOUTH JERSEY

Leonard F. Vernon and Allen Meyers

ARCADIA
PUBLISHING

Published by Arcadia Publishing
Charleston SC, Chicago IL, Portsmouth NH, San Francisco CA

Printed in the United States of America

Library of Congress Catalog Card Number: 2006940200

For all general information contact Arcadia Publishing at:
Telephone 843-853-2070
Fax 843-853-0044
E-mail sales@arcadiapublishing.com
For customer service and orders:
Toll-Free 1-888-313-2665

Visit us on the Internet at www.arcadiapublishing.com

For Sandie, Aislinn, Shayna, Jeffrey, Rachel, and Alyssa,
all of who make my world.

—Leonard F. Vernon

CONTENTS

ACKNOWLEDGMENTS

Although the cover of this book bares my name as the author, it is really the result of a collaboration of individuals who were willing to take time from their lives to assist me in bringing this project to fruition. They include unofficial county historians, librarians, and family members of long-deceased individuals who were willing to go into the attic and search for both photographs as well as relevant information that they thought might be helpful. To all of them, my sincere thanks.

I would like to extend a special thank-you to Phil Cohen, whose knowledge of early Camden, especially its Jewish past, is extensive. Phil was always available to answer any questions I had and was a very valuable asset in assisting me with my fact-checking of the information regarding the city of Camden, both past and present. The process of producing a book consisting of a photographic collection is much more difficult than it might appear. One reason is that previously published information must still be fact-checked, a process that is often ignored by the authors of photographic publications. There is a tendency to accept the previously printed information as fact, when the truth is that there is a continued reprinting of misinformation. This became abundantly clear when researching synagogues in New Jersey, where on more than one occasion a single building was known by various names. This was again pointed out to me by Ruth Bogutz, who served for many years as the president of the Tri-County Jewish Historical Society, who was extremely helpful by stressing that I check and recheck facts before putting them to paper.

Other individuals without whose help I could not have produced this publication are the family of the late Rabbi Abel Respes, Nan Wallace of the Philadelphia Jewish Archives Center, and Leonard Wasserman, whose knowledge of the farming communities of Alliance and Rosenhayn was extremely helpful. A large, heartfelt thank-you to the staff of the Camden County Historical Society, which was extremely helpful and cooperative in assisting me in the making of this book, is also very much in order.

—Leonard F. Vernon

INTRODUCTION

Although Israel has always been the Promised Land, for thousands of Jews fleeing persecution over the past 150 years, southern New Jersey has been home. Jewish life in this region started in the mid-19th century in Trenton, Mercer County, and migrated 175 miles south to Wildwood, Cape May County. The area became home to immigrant Jews from central–eastern Europe, where persecution and survival was a personal choice of life over death for entire extended families. The journey to America and the initial settlements in the Garden State offered a safe haven to reconstitute a sense of family and opportunity to practice one's religious beliefs without fear of government-sponsored violence or pogroms.

The initial development of Jewish life in South Jersey came under the influence of the Philadelphia Jewish community, which dated back to the pre–Revolutionary War era of the 1740s. Easy access to Trenton from Philadelphia developed with the invention of the steam engine railroad era, 100 years later in the 1840s. German Jews arrived en masse to Philadelphia and migrated out of the city northward and across the river to New Jersey for economic opportunities. A group of these enlightened German Jews who yearned to celebrate their newfound religious freedom founded the first synagogue in Trenton, Har Sinai Reform Congregation of Trenton, in 1857.

The next wave of German and eastern European Jews arrived in the middle of the Industrial Revolution and the start of the Iron Age in the 1870s. Again Trenton led the way, with Jews from central Europe flocking to the city that boasted, "What Trenton makes, the World takes." The southern counties of Atlantic and Cape May remained rural and difficult to settle due to their topography. Atlantic County bragged about a community that had a long and open view of the ocean with the founding of Atlantic City, in 1854. The arrival of Jews from Philadelphia in the 1880s made this a popular destination with the completion of a direct route originating from Philadelphia by taking a ferry to Camden and then boarding passenger trains powered by steam locomotives. The trip took an hour to Atlantic City, where urban folks could cool off from the summer heat and humidity.

Atlantic City was known as the "Lungs of Philadelphia." German Jews founded Reform Congregation Beth Israel in the late 1880s with the help of Philadelphia's Reform Congregation Rodeph Sholom.

During this era, Russian Jews were encouraged to journey across the Atlantic Ocean with the lure of a deed to newly built houses with 15 acres and one cow in farming colonies populated by other fellow Jews, deep in Cumberland, Salem, and Cape May Counties during the 1880s–1890s. Passage to America was guaranteed, provided one accepted the conditions and transport from New York City south into South Jersey via steam trains to destinations such as Alliance, Norma, Carmel, Garton Road, Rosenhayn, Monroeville, and the first Jewish self-governed community since biblical times, Woodbine.

The Philadelphia and New York Jewish communities provided aid and support with the help of the Baron de Hirsch Fund and other philanthropic agencies that sought to spread out the massive waves of eastern European Jews from the urban centers with the help of the Jewish

Agricultural Society and Hebrew Immigrant Aid Society (HIAS). The individual Jewish communities flourished in a land where tree stumps were cleared with the new invention of dynamite by the DuPont family in Delaware. The age of the clothing and canning factories supplemented these communities in the off-growing season with jobs and income.

The regular ferry service that connected Philadelphia with its sister city, Camden, across the deep and wide Delaware River started another chapter of American Jewish history in the early 1890s. The stationing of revered Rabbi Naftali Riff by Grand Rabbi Bernard Leventhal of Philadelphia enabled the growth of an Orthodox community of eastern European Jews. The community spread out in two directions along Broadway and Kaighn Avenues with small shops and merchants of all kinds.

As a railroad hub, Camden allowed Jewish settlement along the West Jersey Railroad north to small towns alongside the Delaware River into Burlington and Gloucester Counties. These hardy settlers attained fluency in the English language rapidly and served a great need in their respective towns of Riverside, Burlington, and Mount Holly in the north and Gloucester City, Woodbury, Clayton, Paulsboro, and Pennsgrove in the south. Family and friends extended across state lines into Pennsylvania and Delaware to conduct commercial dealings as iterant merchants and later as shopkeepers.

The end of one generation seemed to find Jews clinging to agricultural and merchant lifestyles by the 1930s. Education and the opportunity to become a professional such as a doctor, lawyer, or dentist allowed these communities to continue after World War I. An example of this evolution is the Browns Mill Sanatorium for Consumptive Diseases started by Jews in 1916 and later known as Deborah Lung and Heart Hospital in Burlington County.

The unfolding of world events such as the Holocaust, World War II, and the birth of the State of Israel added to the vitality of the Jewish communities of South Jersey in the 1950s. Holocaust survivors found chicken farming a means to a livelihood in Vineland, Dorothy, and English Creek.

Post–World War II development and population shifts meant that Jews became part of suburban America as they migrated from Camden to Cherry Hill and from Atlantic City down beach to Margate in the 1960s.

A unique chapter in American Jewish history opened in the early 1960s when a group of African Americans under the spiritual guidance of Rabbi Abel Respes transferred his flock of followers from North Philadelphia to rural Elwood in Galloway Township near Hammonton. This historic move came during the civil rights movement in America that found both black and Jewish urban dwellers moving from initial, second-generation, and third-settlement areas to newer neighborhoods.

Today the American Jewish communities of South Jersey are still evolving and moving to new fourth-settlement areas such as Windsor in Mercer County, Mount Laurel in Burlington County, and East Cherry Hill and Voorhees in Camden County. Migration from Margate onto the mainland in the Northfield area and the enlargement of a Jewish presence in Washington Township, Gloucester County, is a sign of healthy growth and development due to new interstate roads and technological advancements in society that allow for Jews to live farther away from their traditional urban moorings.

Leonard F. Vernon
Allen Meyers

While every effort has been made to verify the accuracy of the information that accompanies the photographs in this book, there have been occasions during the research process where discrepancies appeared. This is especially true with very early photographs where the dates and names would differ from one source to another. In an effort to correct future editions of the book, please feel free to contact Dr. Leonard F. Vernon at (856) 222-1322 with any errors or additional information you may have.

One

ATLANTIC AND CAPE MAY COUNTIES

In the late 19th century, in an effort to rescue fellow Jews from increasing anti-Semitism in czarist Russia, Jewish farming communities were established throughout southern New Jersey

Due to overcrowding in the slums of New York and Philadelphia, where anti-immigrant feelings were starting to run high, the Hebrew Immigrant Aid Society (HIAS), with the assistance of philanthropic foundations such as the Baron de Hirsch Foundation, purchased strips of land, selling them to newly arrived immigrants and financing both their purchase of the land and a home. Expectations were high that these new immigrants could become farmers and thus self-sustaining.

The most ambitious of the Jewish colonies was Woodbine, founded in 1891 from a fund set up by the Baron de Hirsch. Across 2,000 improved acres of upper Cape May County, 12 miles of farm roads and 20 miles of streets, all lit by electricity, were laid.

Intended for both agriculture and small industry, the factory would eventually outdistance the farm as the preference of the Jewish immigrants at Woodbine.

Woodbine's most dramatic accomplishment was the Baron de Hirsch Agricultural School, where nearly 100 students every year were instructed in scientific farming. Among the Woodbine school's most famous graduates was Jacob G. Lipman, who became a director of the Rutgers Experiment Station and, in 1915, was named the first dean of the state university's College of Agriculture.

As a consequence of the anti-Semitism, Jews soon formed their own resorts, and Atlantic City was on of these. Other popular shore towns for Jews in the years between 1891 and 1896 were the communities of Long Branch and Asbury Park.

Not specifically a Jewish resort, Atlantic City would become a welcoming respite for urban Jews seeking a stay by the sea, thus gaining a reputation as a Jewish resort town.

The Jewish population during the summer season in Atlantic City was so high that it began to worry the chamber of commerce of the city. It feared that the large number of Jews would limit the number of non-Jews that visited the city. In an effort to temper this, many hotels established a "Christians Only" policy.

Today old Atlantic City hotels like the Breakers and the Traymore, like the restrictions on Jews they imposed, have long since vanished.

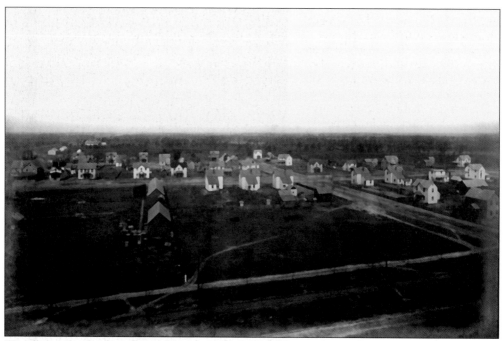

Woodbine was the first all-Jewish town in the United States. One will notice, in this aerial view from the early 1900s, that there are no power lines: electricity was not brought into the town until 1915.

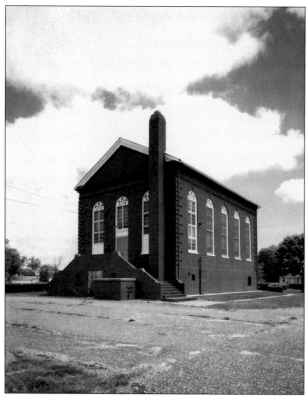

As soon as each family had food on the table and a roof over their heads, they could then turn their attention back to religion. In 1893, the community formed the Brotherhood Congregation and brick by brick began the building of the community's first of an eventual four synagogues. The Baron de Hirsch Foundation lent the community two-thirds of the funds while the residents raised the other one-third.

In 1896, the Brotherhood Synagogue opened its doors to the residents of the community. The synagogue, seen here in 2001, was also known by the name Agudath Achim Anshe; it not only served as a place to pray but as a Hebrew school for the community's children. Additionally Brotherhood Hall, a meeting hall within the building, served as a favorite place for holding meetings.

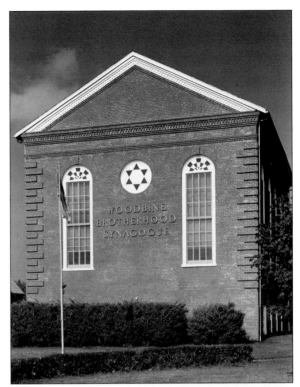

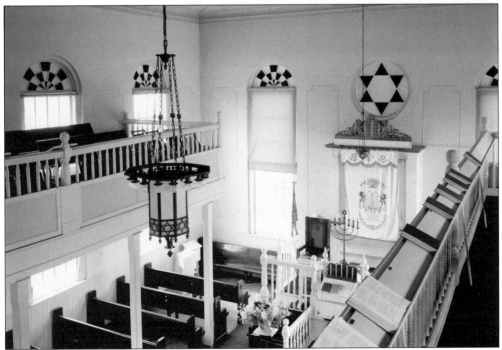

Brotherhood Synagogue was an Orthodox synagogue. Within this branch of Judaism, men and women sat separate from one another. The men sat downstairs while the women sat in the balcony.

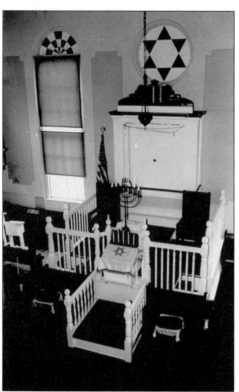

This image displays the interior *aron kodesh* of the Woodbine Brotherhood Synagogue as seen in 2001.

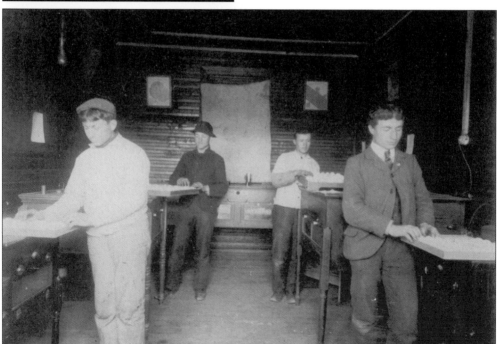

New Jersey would become known as the egg basket of America. In this photograph, students from the Baron de Hirsch Agricultural School in Woodbine separate eggs and prepare them for kindling, which was done by hand.

One of the most prominent families in Woodbine was the Rabinowitzs. This is a photograph of Albert Rabinowitz, a descendent of the original family, taken in April 2001 in front of the Woodbine Brotherhood Synagogue.

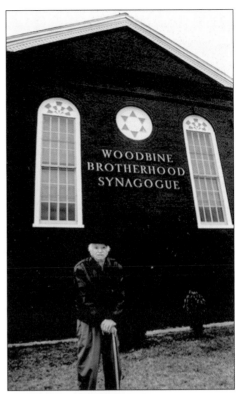

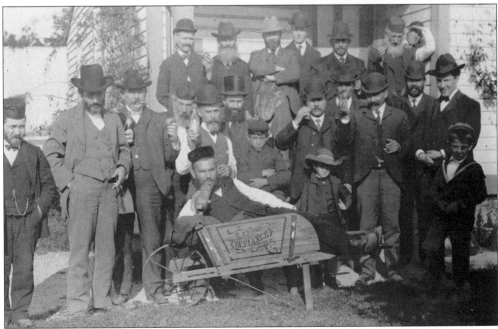

Here a group of Orthodox Jewish men pose for a group photograph during a Simchas Torah Kiddush in Woodbine (around 1910). The writing on the cart spells *defiance* and may have been used as part of a protest against factory owners. Strikes and worker protests would become a common occurrence in Woodbine.

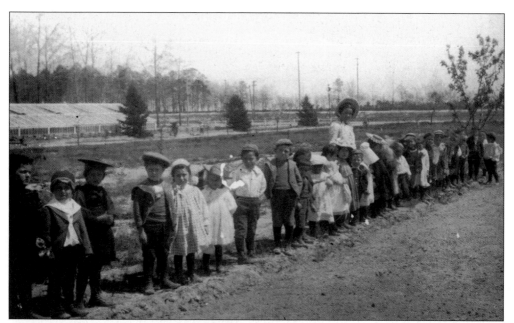

Woodbine parents realized that education was the road to success, and one of the first projects undertaken by the community was the building of a school. Woodbine's first school was built on property donated by the Baron de Hirsch Foundation. In this *c.* 1915 photograph, a group of kindergarten students is seen with its teacher standing outside of the school. Ironically it would be the success of the education that spelled the end of Woodbine as a farming community.

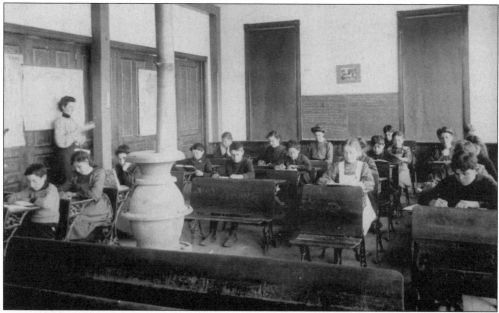

As one can see in this late-1800s photograph, Woodbine students tackled their studies with zeal. Writers who have studied New Jersey's Jewish farming communities have stated that, like other Jewish families, they cherished education, believing that "education was the stepping stone to a larger life." Parents sacrificed in order to build Woodbine's first public school, and when classes became overcrowded, larger schools were constructed.

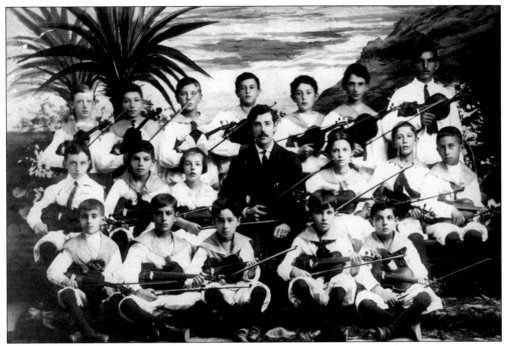

The arts were as important as academics to these immigrant farmers, and the teaching of music was an important part of the overall education of Woodbine children. In this 1912 photograph, Harry Sussman appears with his violin class.

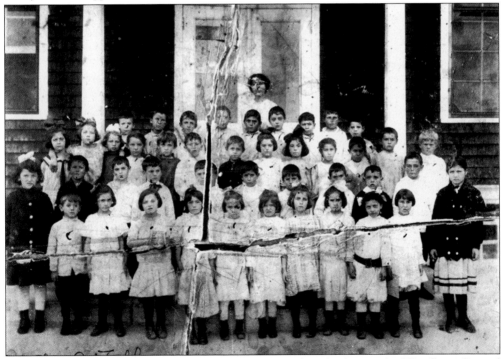

Here is Anna Levenson Stone and her first- and second-grade class at the Woodbine Central School in 1911.

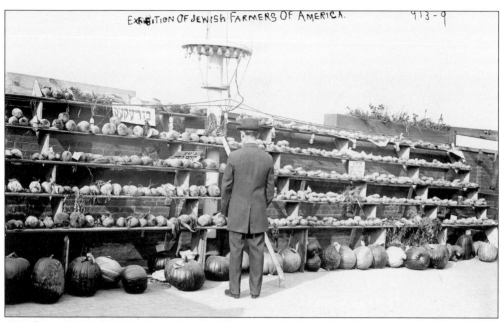

Woodbine farmers would often exhibit at farm shows both in New Jersey and elsewhere in the country. Woodbine's variety of agricultural and industrial products repeatedly captured awards at the Cape May County Fair.

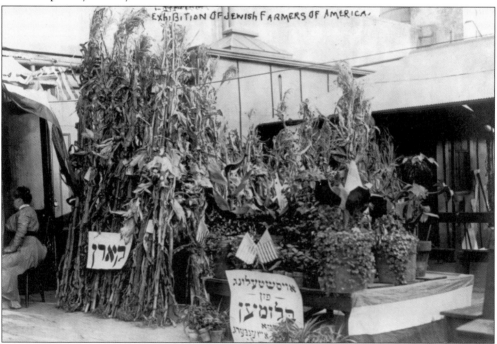

While the quality of the product grown in Woodbine was often criticized by competing farming communities, especially the gentleman farmers of Vineland, this reputation would eventually change. Woodbine crops gained in reputation, eventually entering competitions against other Jewish farm colonies from across the United States, such as the competition sponsored by the Jewish Farmers of America seen in this photograph.

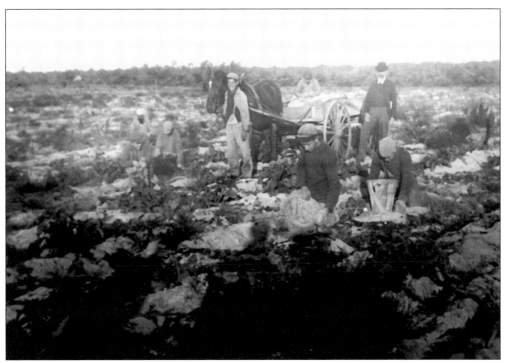

The many crops grown in Woodbine included tomatoes, grapes, peaches, and, as seen here, potatoes.

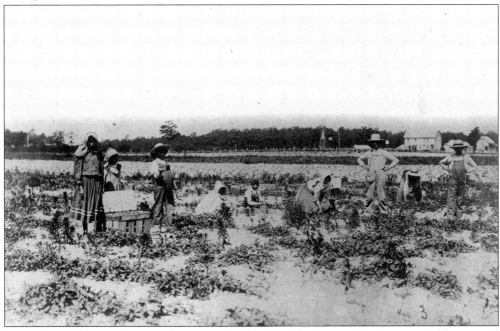

The picking of crops at harvest time was a family affair. Mothers and their young children would often go to other farms in the community and help pick the crops in an effort to make extra money for the family. An example of the pay scale was about 2¢ for every pint of blueberries picked; thus, a mother and child together could earn an extra $3 a day.

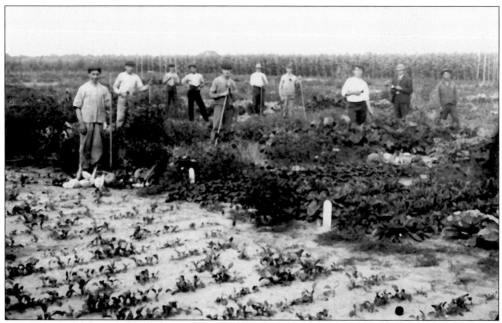

Here Jewish farmers in Woodbine take a minute from working the fields to pose for the camera.

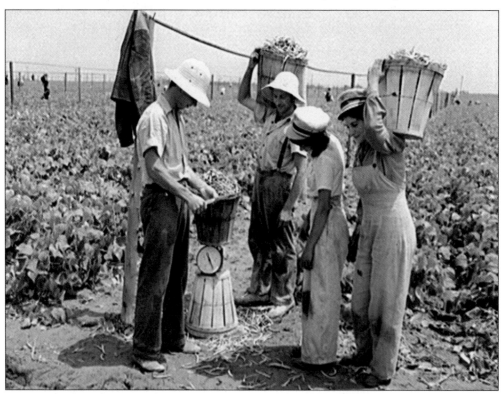

Farming for the colonist was hard work and did not discriminate against women, who when not working in the factories sewing would be in the fields, many times with their children, in an effort to assist their husbands.

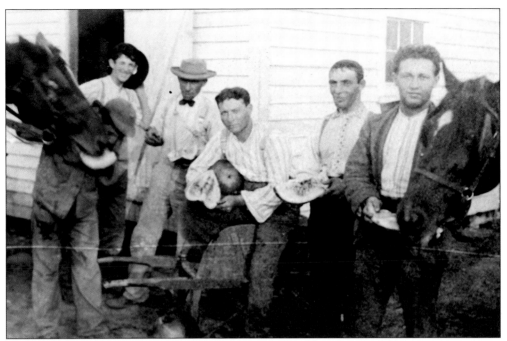

Even with Woodbine's poor soil, crops such as watermelons grew well. There are many stories of Woodbine teenagers sneaking into the watermelon patch and stealing watermelons to crack open and eat the "center meat" and discard the rest. Perhaps that is what these teenagers were up to, one of whom appears to be carrying a large watermelon under his arm.

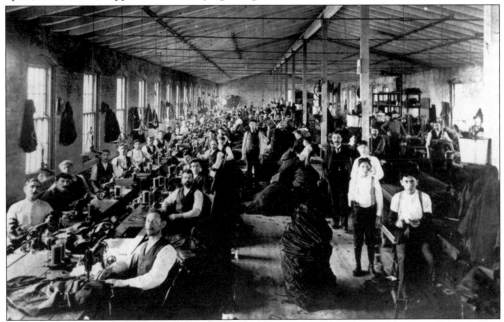

Despite their successes, many residents of Woodbine discovered that farming could not put food on the table. Within 20 years, most people had given up on farming and turned to factory work. Fathers would eventually join their wives and even their children in the various garment factories in the area.

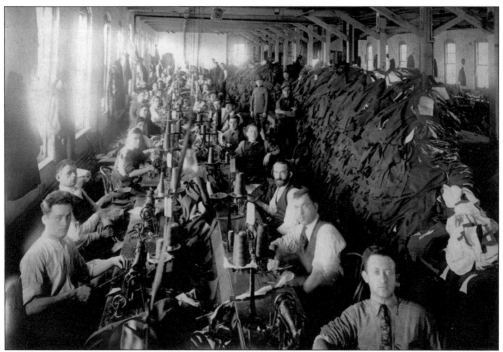

During World War I, the factory switched its production to uniforms for the armed forces; after the war, it returned to manufacturing children's clothing.

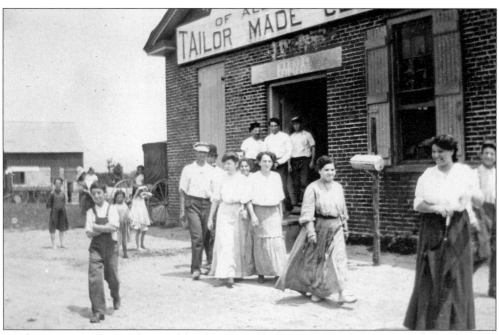

Working in a small-town factory, like the N. Snellenberg's Garment Factory, with good airflow and lighting, beat working in the sweatshops of New York or Philadelphia. The trustees of Woodbine would lure manufactures with incentives such as free rent, housing, and utilities. Eventually the product lines expanded to offer coats, hats, paper boxes, and cigars.

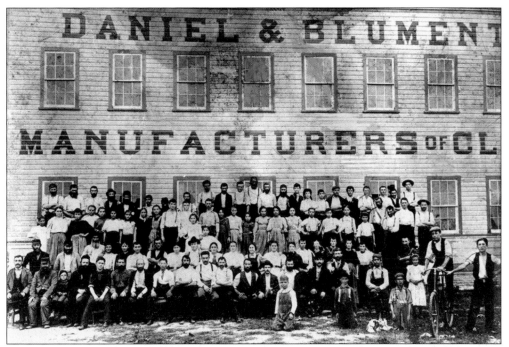

This 1910 photograph is of a children's clothing factory in Woodbine. In 1903, workers walked off at the Daniel and Blumenthal clothing factory in the town's first ever factory strike. Joseph Rabinowitz was the president of the company and a Woodbine resident for 40 years.

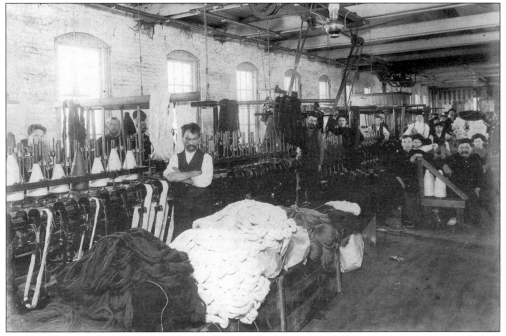

In this photograph is a gentleman who does not look particularly happy; perhaps the hard work from the day has gotten to him, or maybe he is a manager in the plant and feels that the picture taking is disruptive to production since his workers must stop working for the photograph.

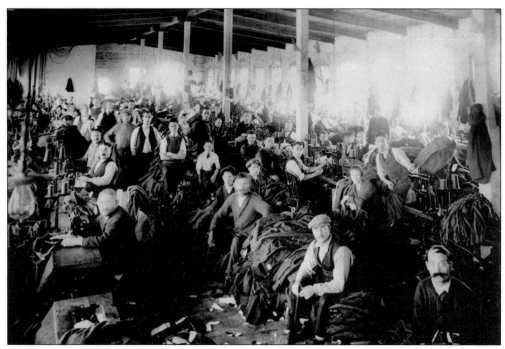

Workers are at their sewing machines in the Daniel and Blumenthal clothing factory.

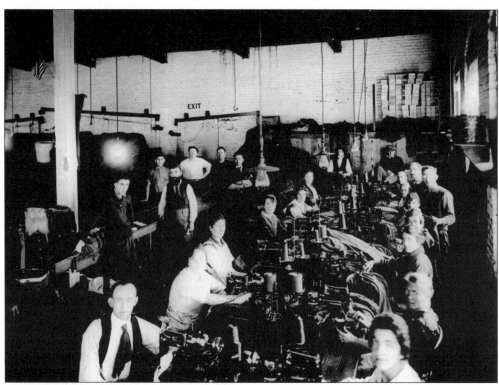

Both men and women toiled at their sewing machines. Since farming was a seasonal occupation, men would join their wives in the garment factories when not planting crops.

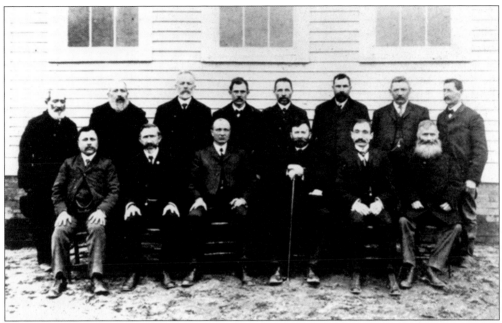

Woodbine was the first Jewish borough incorporated in the United States. This photograph is of the mayor and council in 1910; Joseph Rabinowitz is fifth from the left in the first row. Rabinowitz served as Woodbine's mayor from 1910 to 1920, as well as serving on the Magnolia, Cape May County, city council from 1920 to 1940.

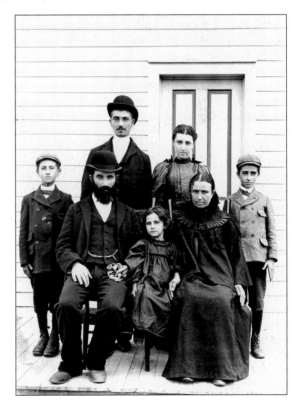

In this c. 1900 photograph is a Russian Jewish family one year after their arrival in Woodbine. The town of Woodbine was established in 1891 by the Baron de Hirsch Fund as part of its program to settle Jewish immigrants in self-sustaining communities. It appears that they may be dressed for Sabbath services.

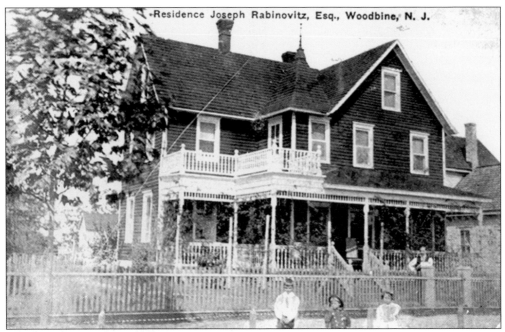

This is a photograph of the Joseph Rabinowitz home. Visible from left to right are Ben, Chester, Zelda, and Joseph Rabinowitz.

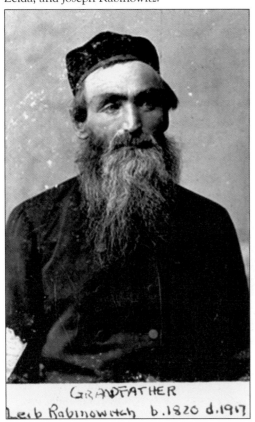

GRANDFATHER
Leib Rabinowitch b.1820 d.1917

This 1891 photograph, taken in Russia, is of Leib Rabinowitz. Leib was the father of Joseph Rabinowitz.

This 1910 photograph is of Leib Rabinowitz, taken upon his arrival in Philadelphia.

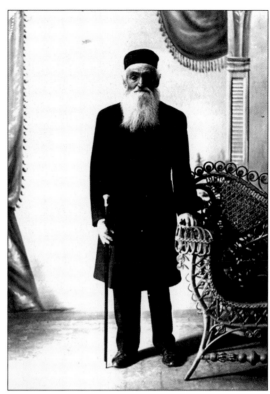

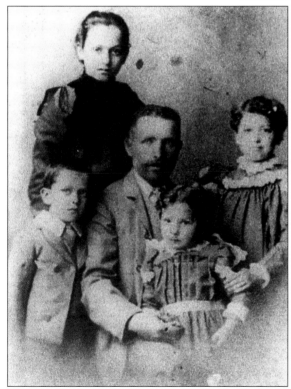

Barnet Silberman served as one of the chief builders/carpenters of Woodbine housing. Shown here with his wife and children, he was born in Minsk, Russia, in 1862. He was proud to say that "here in America it's safe. You can play out of doors."

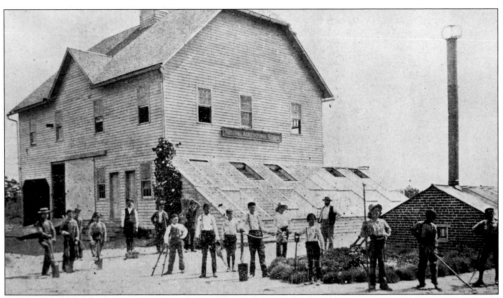

Many settlers were new to farming and even those with some experience were not familiar with growing crops such as blueberries and sweet potatoes, which were common New Jersey crops. In 1898, after increasing community tensions about the lack of instruction in growing New Jersey crops as well as farming in general, the Baron de Hirsch Agricultural School (also known as Woodbine Agricultural School) was opened. By 1902, there were 160 students, mainly boys. The school provided education by using practical experience on the school's demonstration farms. Here a group of students is receiving instruction in farming technique. Behind them the sign on the building reads Woodbine Agricultural School.

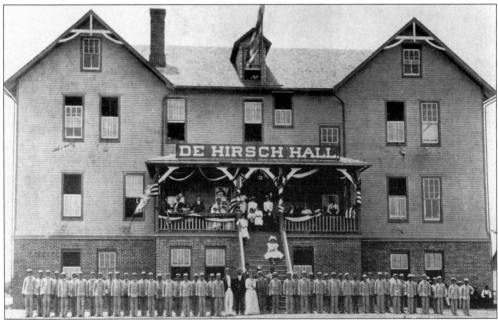

De Hirsch Hall was a social hall in Woodbine. It was named after the Jewish philanthropist Baron Maurice de Hirsch. The children seen here in uniform are students of the Baron de Hirsch Agricultural School posing following a parade, possibly a Fourth of July celebration.

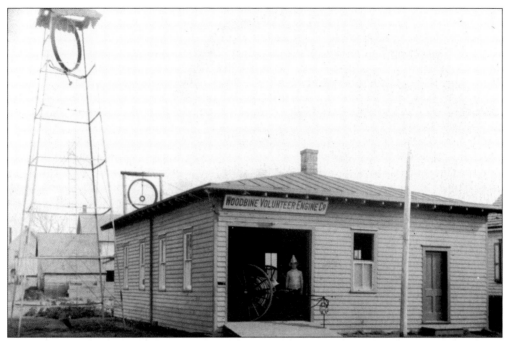

This photograph shows the firehouse located in Woodbine. Next to the firehouse is the alarm tower.

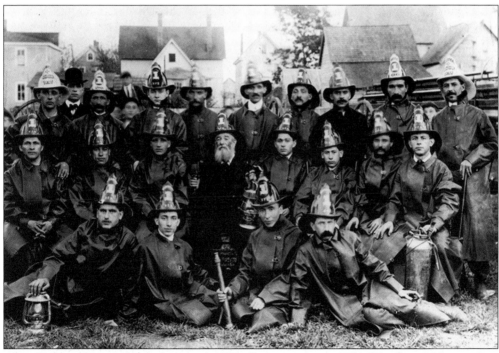

This photograph was taken in 1910 in the Woodbine community. The Woodbine Volunteer Fire Department, incorporated in 1902, was in charge of all emergencies in the community. Among those pictured here is Lou Shapiro, a resident of Woodbine. The man in the center with the beard is the fire chief.

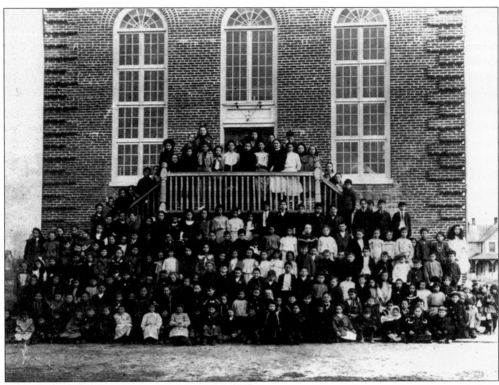

Here a group of Woodbine Central School students pose for a photograph in front of their school building around 1910.

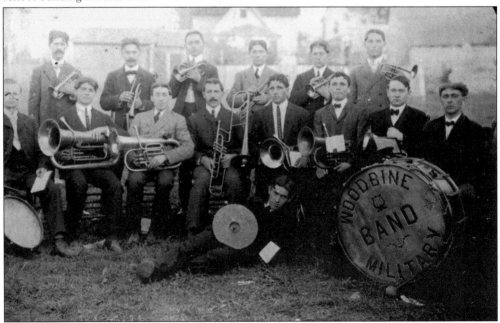

The Woodbine Military Band played for high school athletic events. Members of the Woodbine basketball team would call signals to one another in Yiddish in an effort to confuse their opponents.

Jewish philanthropist Baron de Hirsch and his foundation were the financial support behind the Woodbine colony. Eventually the agricultural school, as well as other buildings in the township of Woodbine, would bare his name.

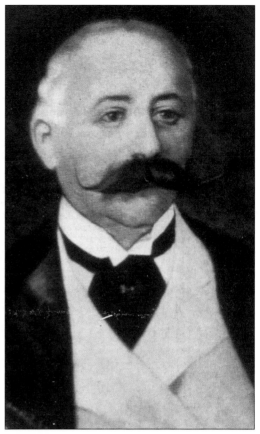

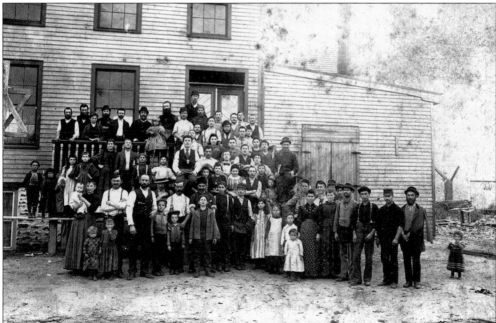

This *c.* 1910 photograph shows residents of Woodbine posing for a group portrait.

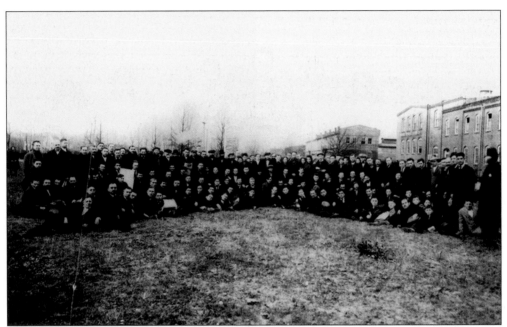

Workers pose for this 1910 photograph. They are probably employed in the manufacturing factory seen in the rear of the photograph.

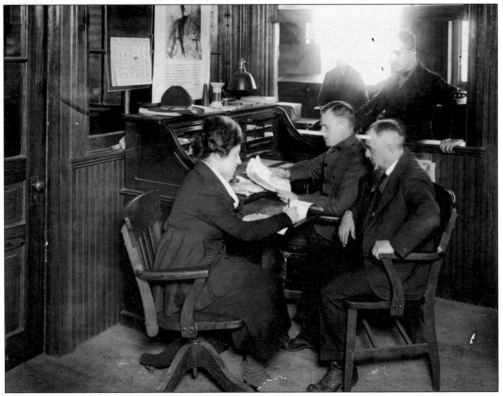

This photograph taken in 1916 shows the officers of the Woodbine Children's Clothing Factory discussing business.

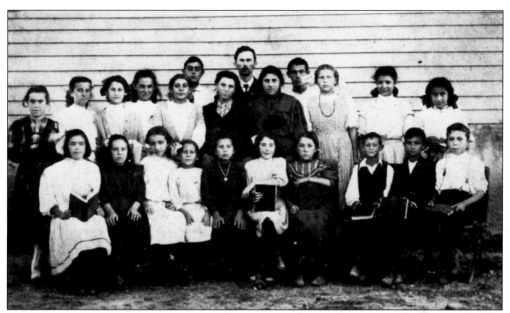

A Mr. Carlisle and his class at the Woodbine School are seen here.

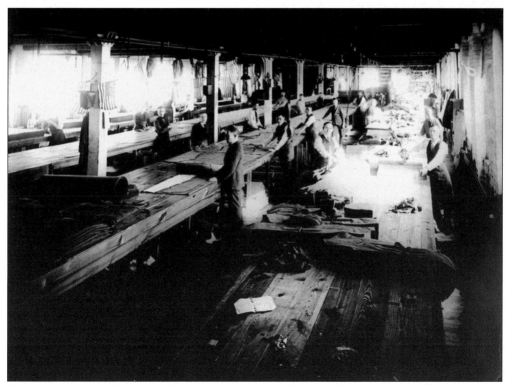

This 1910 photograph shows the interior of a manufacturing factory in Woodbine. Working conditions were harsh and ventilation poor.

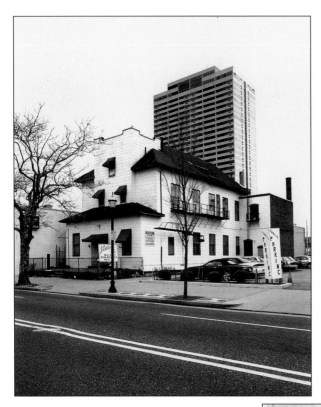

The organization Preservation New Jersey has listed Beth Israel Synagogue as one of the 10 Most Endangered Historic Sites in New Jersey. Located in Atlantic City, Atlantic County, it was built in 1872, Beth Israel was the town's first Jewish house of worship and today is one of the oldest synagogue buildings in New Jersey. Its continued presence is an important reminder of the Jewish influence in Atlantic City.

Architecturally Beth Israel is an unusual structure, combining Moorish Revival and shingle-style elements. The building was converted to apartments in the 1930s. Efforts to save the building continue, and although the building reportedly needs some structural repair, most of the changes that have occurred are reversible.

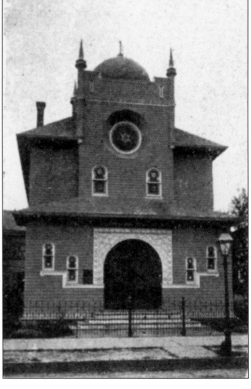

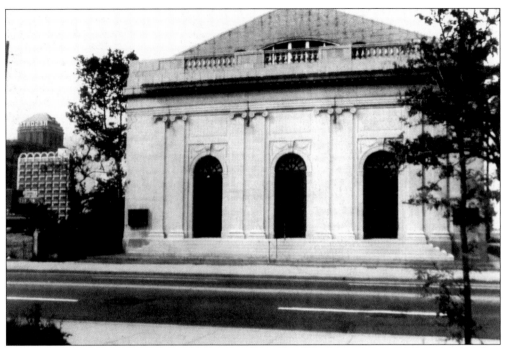

Although the old Beth Israel Synagogue was sill usable, the growing congregation decided that it needed a larger home and in 1913 built this mausoleum-like structure at 906 Pacific Avenue in Atlantic City.

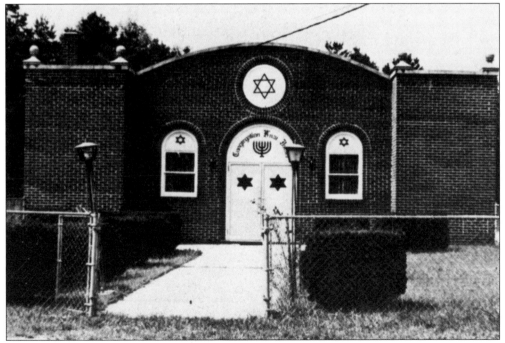

B'nai Israel Farmers Congregation, located in English Creek, was founded by Holocaust survivors who came to America from displaced persons camps after the conclusion of World War II. The congregation was made up of mostly chicken farmers in the nearby community.

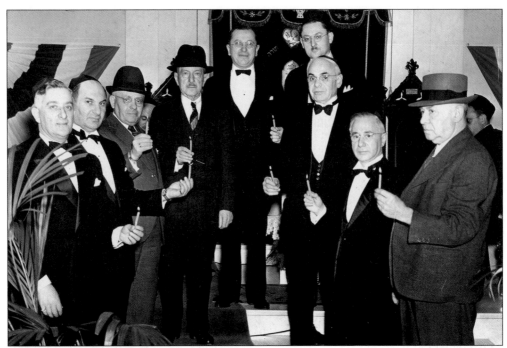

Rabbi Moshe Shapiro (fourth from the right), with officers of Congregation Rodef Sholom, celebrate a major milestone in the synagogue's history, the burning of its mortgage in the early 1950s. The synagogue was located at 2016 Pacific Avenue, Atlantic City.

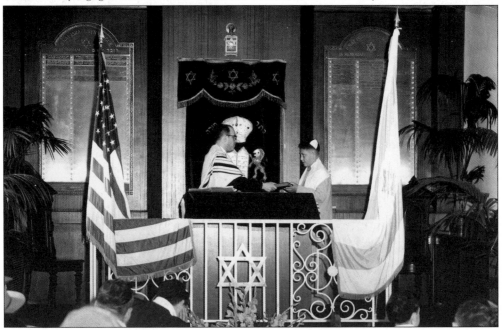

The rite of passage in Judaism comes at the early age of 13, when a male is welcomed into the total community and is delegated rights and responsibilities. The bar mitzvah ceremony is the first step that leads to adult life and allows for the young man to be counted as part of minyan and the call to prayer, which requires 10 people.

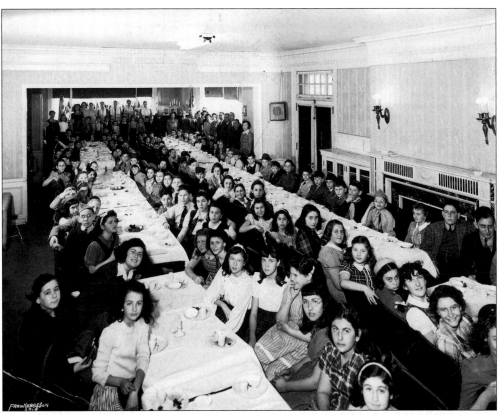

The Atlantic City Jewish community, post World War II, created the institution of the Free Hebrew School of Atlantic City located in the Rodef Sholom Synagogue on Pacific Avenue. Children from as far away as Pleasantville were shuttled by volunteers after school for their Jewish education.

CONGREGATION RODEF SHOLOM

4609 ATLANTIC AVENUE   ::   ATLANTIC CITY, N. J. 08401

Kindly offer special prayers אל מלא רחמים **in memory of my deceased**

....

....

MAY THEIR SOULS REST IN PEACE

I am donating to the Congregation $..

Name..

Address..

This Card is a Record of my Ideals

There can be no finer tribute to your departed than a contribution in their memory to the Synagogue.

During High Holiday services, the traditional appeal was followed by a voice pledge to honor one's father and mother, if deceased. Since no money could be transacted during a holiday, this "Yiskor Card" was sent in along with the pledge money after the holiday.

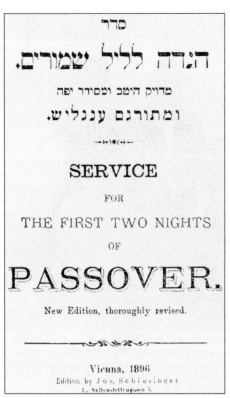

סדר

הַגָּדָה לְלֵיל שִׁמּוּרִים.

מדויק היטב ומסודר יפה

וּמְתוּרְגָם עֶנְגְלִישׁ.

SERVICE

FOR

THE FIRST TWO NIGHTS

OF

PASSOVER.

New Edition, thoroughly revised.

Vienna, 1896
Edition by Jos. Schlesinger
I., Seitenstettengasse 5.

The Jewish population of Gloucester City was bolstered in number in the early 1930s by Jews who escaped Hitler's Germany. They arrived with traditions in hand and carried religious books, including a Passover Haggadah like the one seen here.

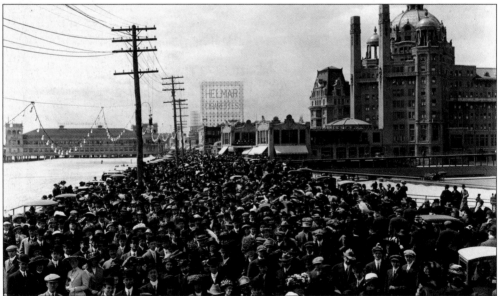

Because of its easy accessibility and variety of amusements, Atlantic City became a magnet for masses of German Jewish families and later waves of eastern European vacationers. Atlantic City became one of the most popular vacation spots for Jews living in East Coast cities; however, the welcome mat was not extended by all to Jews. In the background of this 1911 photograph is the Blenheim Hotel. By the 1930s, it, as well as many other beach hotel brochures, included a warning that accommodations were reserved for "Christian Gentiles."

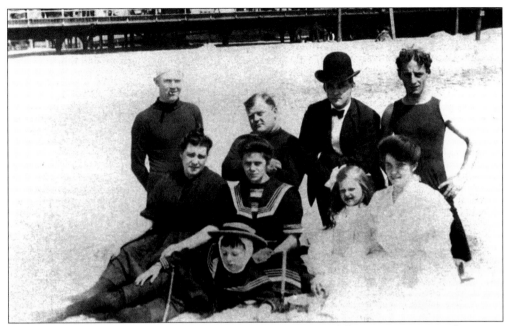

During the summer, a local reporter observed, "There are now fully 75,000 visitors at the resort, and it is safe to say that of this grand total fully one-third are Israelites. They are the resort's best and most steadfast patrons." A family is seen here on the beach in full clothing, which was the custom of the day. By law, men were able to bare the arms and a portion of their legs.

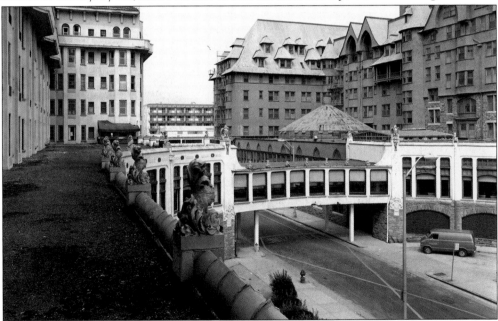

This is a photograph of the Marlborough-Blenheim Hotels with the Sun Gallery Bridge. The bridge, which joined the two hotels, spanned Ohio Avenue. The increase in anti-Semitism in Cape May during the 1890s, with Jews being excluded from hotels, clubs, and neighborhoods in Cape May, caused a migration to other shore resorts between 1891 and 1896, where they formed their own Jewish resorts in places such as Atlantic City, Long Branch, and Asbury Park.

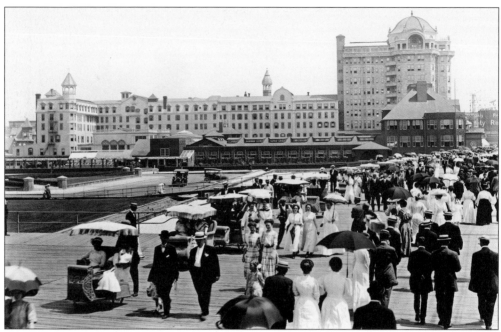

Crowds of fashionable Jewish visitors from all the nearby cities were a fixture of Atlantic City's high-society summer scene. People would walk or be wheeled in special chairs on the boardwalk. Atlantic City became the resort of choice among well-to-do families such as the Hutzlers, Bambergers, and Sonneborns of Baltimore. The Hotel Traymore, seen in the background, was blatantly anti-Semitic until 1945 when it would welcome "all white patrons" with enough money to pay for a room and three meals a day. Dating to 1870, the Atlantic City Boardwalk was originally a walkway to the ocean, as opposed to running alongside it. The change was prompted by concerns about sand—hotel owners were upset about it being tracked into their establishments.

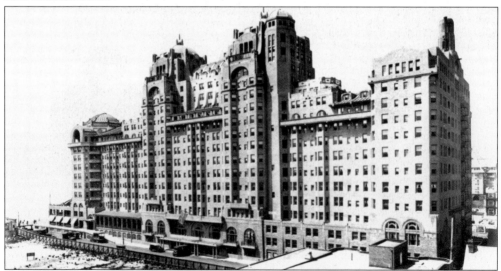

This is a close-up of the Hotel Traymore. The hotel was one of many on the Atlantic City Boardwalk that restricted Jews from being guests. Eventually the restrictions would be lifted and Jews of prominence and wealth were allowed to stay in the hotel.

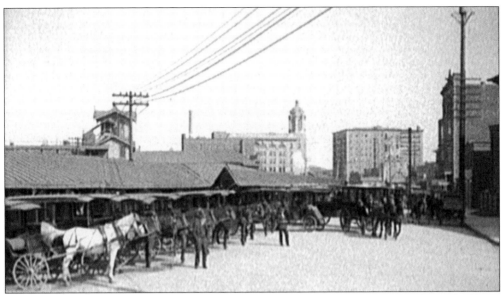

In 1850, the undeveloped land that was to become Atlantic City had only seven households. In this same year, Dr. Jonathan Pitney decided that Atlantic City's proximity to the shore would make a suitable destination for the ill. Pitney and civil engineer Richard B. Osborne, as well as various businessmen from Philadelphia, started a train route from Camden to Atlantic City, connecting people from Philadelphia and other mid-Atlantic cities to the new resort. The rail service began in 1854. In this image is one of the very early hotels with its horse-drawn limousine, which would carry patrons from the railroad station to the hotel.

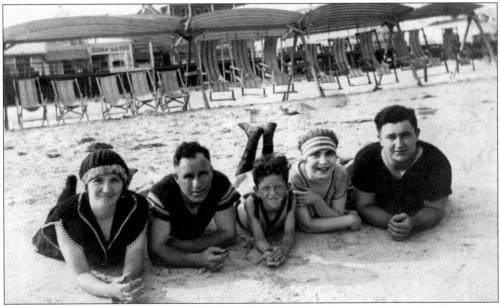

Atlantic City would become one of the largest Jewish playgrounds because by the 1890s Jews were being excluded from hotels, clubs, and neighborhoods in Cape May, although nearby Wildwood remained somewhat friendly to Jews. This 1917 photograph shows a Jewish family enjoying a day at the beach. Although, one has to wonder how enjoyable it could have been with the required cover-ups of the day.

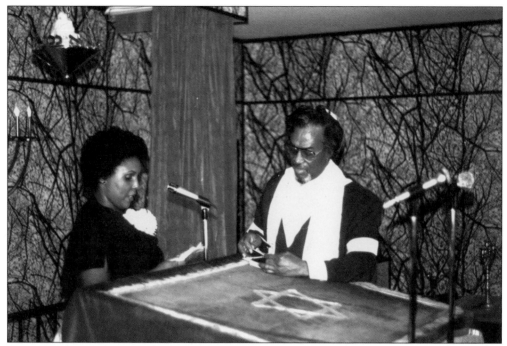

One of Atlantic County's lesser known congregations was Temple Adat Beyt Moshe. The congregation's spiritual leader was Rabbi Abel Respes, who founded this all-Black congregation in Philadelphia in 1951. In 1962, the congregation moved to Elwood in Atlantic County and chose to live communally. Unlike many of the "black Hebrew" congregations in Philadelphia and New York, Respes's congregation underwent a formal conversion to Judaism in 1971. Rabbi Respes is seen here on the bema (altar) of the Adat Beyt Moshe synagogue with his daughter-in-law.

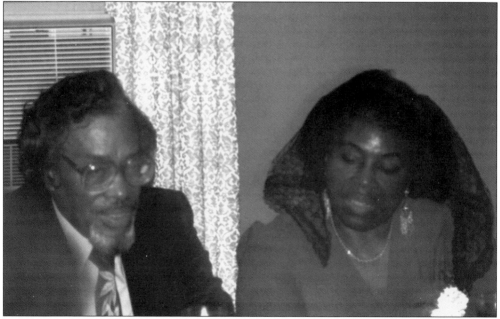

Seen are Rabbi Respes and his wife at a Shabbat dinner in the Respes home.

Two

SALEM, CUMBERLAND, AND GLOUCESTER COUNTIES

In addition to the Woodbine colony, there were other Jewish farming communities developed in New Jersey. The colony of Alliance, located in Salem County, about 43 miles southeast of Philadelphia and 4 miles from Vineland, served as a market-town for the farmers of the colony.

The colony was named after the Alliance Israélite Universelle, which provided the funds for its foundation. The colony's first families were brought there in May 1882 and were temporarily housed in three large wooden buildings. The sandy bush and scrub oak soil, common in southern New Jersey, was not very conducive to farming, causing the settlers to begin their new journey at a distinct disadvantage.

At the outset, 25 families, principally from cities of southern Russia (Elizabethgrad, Odessa, Kiev, and so on), settled at Alliance; this number soon increased to 67 families. Housed in the three crowded temporary buildings, the colonists survived the first winter with help in part by the HIAS. The next year the land was divided into 15-acre farms; houses consisting of two rooms and a cellar were erected, wells sunk, and other improvements made.

Each farmer entered into a contract, which was to be paid within 10 years. In the contract the farmer promised to repay $350 for his holding, the house being reckoned at $150. The number of acres devoted to communal purposes, school buildings, factories, burial grounds, and so on, was 150.

Manufacturing would eventually be introduced into the colony, at first on a small scale, later increasing. The success of the Alliance settlement prompted the establishment of the nearby towns of Norma, Brotmanville, Rosenhayn, and Carmel for Russian and Polish Jews.

The Jewish colonies looked to Cumberland County, specifically Vineland, for a market for their produce. Soon members of the Jewish communities moved to Vineland to open stores and a variety of other commercial establishments.

As industry advanced, the farms were deserted. Factories in Alliance and Rosenhayn were transferred to Vineland, where there was a larger labor supply. By the end of the 19th century, the city had a sizeable Jewish population, which at mid-20th century had expanded to 1,200 families.

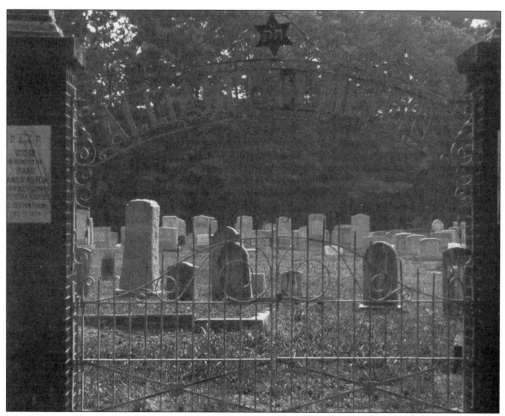

This photograph shows the front entrance to the Alliance Cemetery with its dedication. The cemetery is dedicated to the founders of Alliance. Many of the colony's original settlers are interred here along with other Jewish residents of the surrounding farm colonies of southern New Jersey.

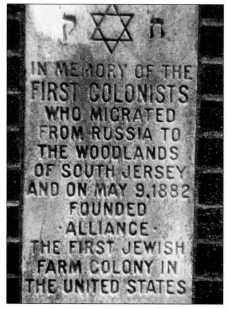

IN MEMORY OF THE FIRST COLONISTS WHO MIGRATED FROM RUSSIA TO THE WOODLANDS OF SOUTH JERSEY AND ON MAY 9, 1882 FOUNDED · ALLIANCE · THE FIRST JEWISH FARM COLONY IN THE UNITED STATES

An inscription on the Alliance Cemetery gate bears a dedication to the colony's founders.

The Alliance Cemetery Mortuary houses the former synagogue furnishings from Brotmanville. Today it serves as both a Jewish museum and a mortuary.

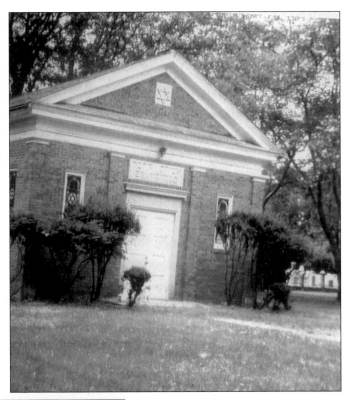

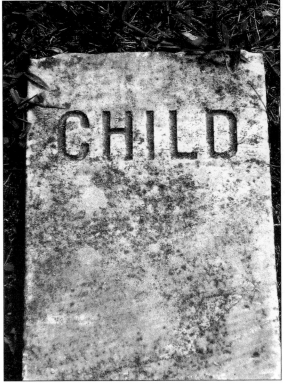

Headstones simply stating the word *child* were unfortunately a familiar scene in the Alliance Cemetery. Many of the resolute pioneers lost children through a combination of early hardships, including strenuous work in the fields, inadequate nutrition, and the prevalent "milk sickness." This mysterious disease was highly fatal, killing many children during numerous reported outbreaks in Alliance.

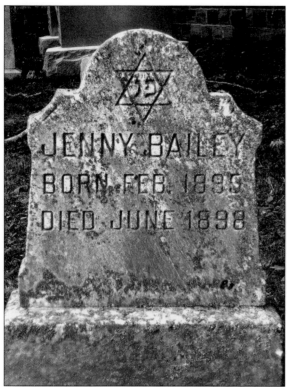

This is a headstone bearing the name of a three-year-old child in the Alliance Cemetery. In the mid-20th century, researchers finally confirmed that "milk sickness" was caused by a poison produced by the white snakeroot plant. Grazing animals, such as cows and goats, ate the plant and passed the toxin to humans through milk and meat. Improved farming practices drastically reduced incidence rates of the disease, while modern medical research found a cure for the infected. When the last recorded cases among humans occurred in 1963, the patients were quickly restored to health.

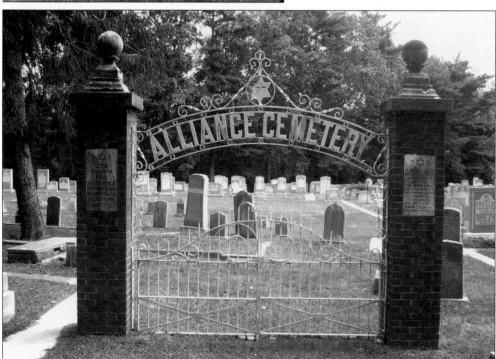

In this view of the entrance to the cemetery, one can see the dedication inscriptions on each of the two pillars.

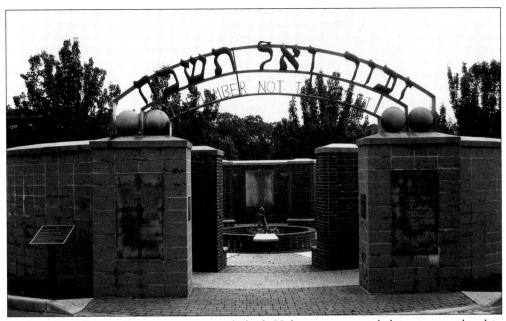

Within the Alliance Cemetery is a recently built Holocaust memorial that was completed in 1995. There is a dedication wall as well as a fountain in the center of the memorial.

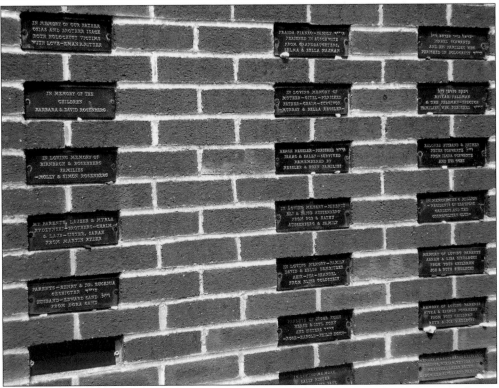

Within the memorial is a dedication wall. Friends and relatives can purchase plaques to honor a loved one who either perished during the Holocaust or was a survivor who passed away while in the United States.

45

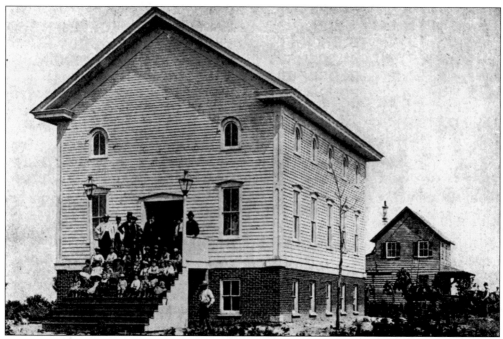

The cornerstone for the first synagogue in Alliance was laid on the first day of Chanukah, Sunday, December 11, 1887. The two-story building was constructed with a stone foundation, brick, and clapboard. Residents could not agree on a name for the congregation. Traditionalists called it Eban Ha' Ezer (the Rock of Deliverance), while the newspaper the *Jewish Exponent* referred to it as Congregation Emanu-El.

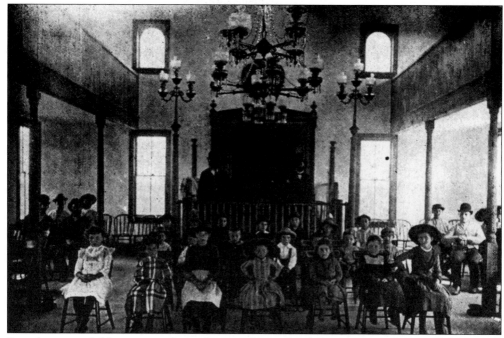

Seen here are children posing for a photograph inside of Congregation Emanu-El (Eban Ha' Ezer) synagogue.

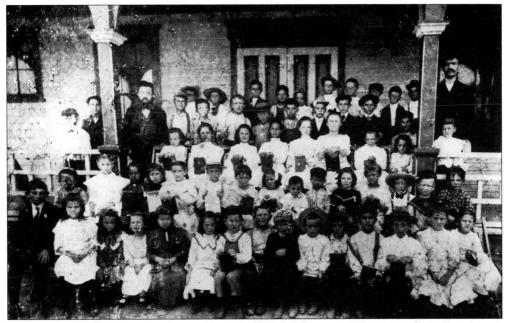

Jewish education continued to be important to settlers, who passed down Jewish traditions both in the home and through Hebrew school classes. This is a 1905 photograph of a Talmud Torah (Hebrew school) class for the children of Alliance colony.

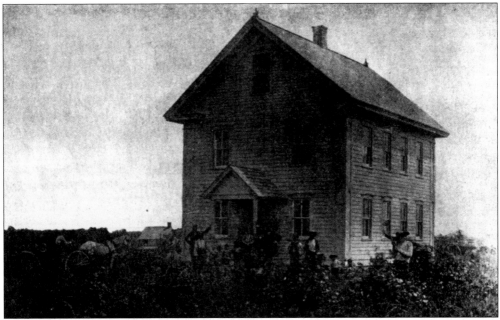

The second synagogue built in Alliance, albeit to considerably less fanfare, opened in 1884–1885. Tiphereth Israel (Glory of Israel) Congregation, later renamed Shearith Israel (Remnant of Israel), resembled a large house, except for the two extended windows on the gable end. Thus the colony had built two synagogues within its first decade of existence. Tiphereth Israel, unlike Emanu-El, was used exclusively for worship and study, while Emanu-El was used for social events as well as worship.

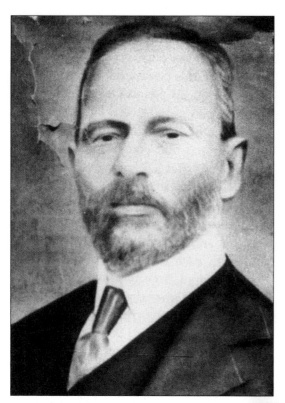

Hirsh Coltun and his family were among the founding families of the Alliance colony.

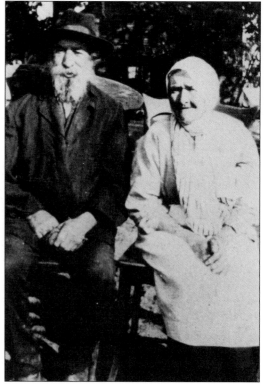

The Crystal family was among the original Alliance residents. Raphael Crystal, seen here with his wife, Martha, in his later years, was one of the first Alliance farmers to plant what were considered luxury crops, such as asparagus. Raphael taught himself how to do this by reading agricultural publications. Their son Jacob would later purchase land next to his father's farm and would become an influential part of the community for many years. He is unique in being one of the very few second-generation Alliance residents to continue in farming.

In 1916, in an effort to demonstrate the power of its new explosive, the DuPont Company blasted the tree trunks that still remained after 20 years on Jacob Crystal's farm. Most children of the pioneer Alliance farmers did not stay on the farm after marriage, school, or attaining professional status. Thus the efforts of Alliance parents to stress education became both a blessing as well as a curse to the community. Jacob Crystal (seen here in front of a crop dusting plane with his wife) was the exception to this flight from the community.

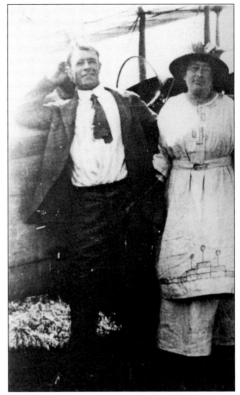

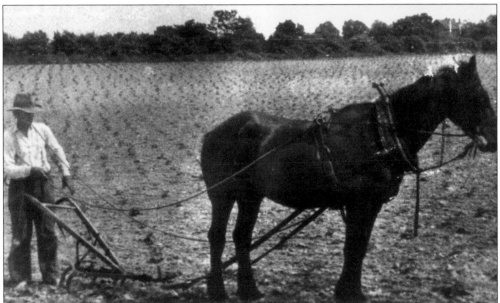

The ideological roots of the American Jewish agricultural colonies can be traced to the Am Olam, an organization that advocated communal agrarian settlements by Jews in the United States. Among the large number of original colonists who had Am Olam connections were the Steinbergs. In this early image is Harry Steinberg, plowing his Alliance colony farm with his horses.

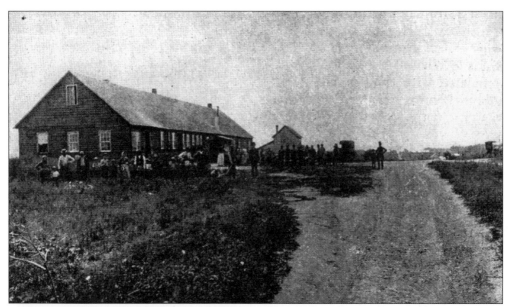

In May and June 1882, 400 immigrants, including 160 children, were brought by train to Alliance. They were taken to what they described as a barracks, which was known as Castle Garden in mock honor of New York's famed depot. The barracks was divided into rooms just large enough for a bed, chair, and small table. Communal living continued until individual houses on the land were completed. By 1883, the population of Alliance had grown to over 650, a great many of these still living in communal arrangements.

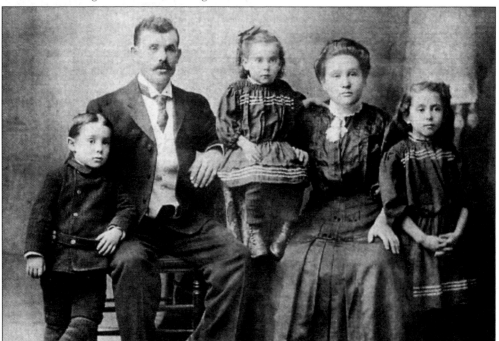

The Fisher family is seen in this c. 1907 picture, shortly after their arrival in the United States from Kiev, Ukraine. Nathan, Max, Bess, Pearl, and Ida, from left to right, would eventually settle in Bridgeton.

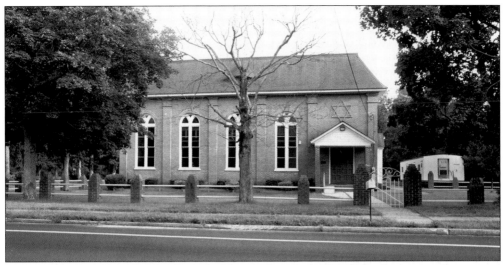

Beth Hillel Synagogue of Carmel, another farm colony in southern New Jersey, was constructed between 1901 and 1907. It was designed by Louis Mounier, a French immigrant to the United States who resided in Vineland, and since its construction, it has been in constant use by the Orthodox Jews of the area, including the present time. It is believed to be the only Orthodox synagogue in South Jersey and in Cumberland County that is still being used regularly throughout the year for religious worship. Beth Hillel is listed on the National Register of Historic Places.

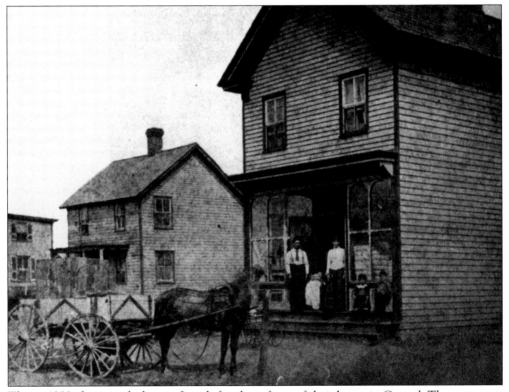

This c. 1889 photograph shows a Jewish family in front of their home in Carmel. The structures were modest in design.

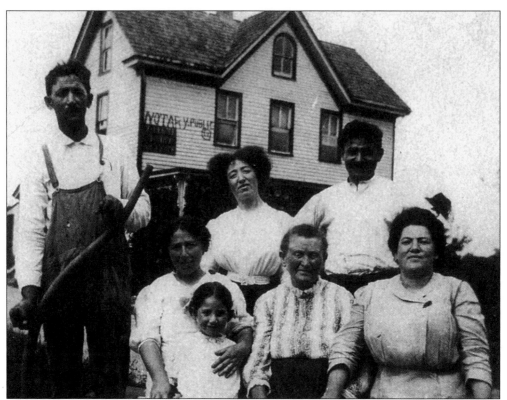

While in Odessa, Russia, a branch of the Am Olam was formed by Sidney Baily and Mordechai Woskoboynokoff. The Woskoboynokoff family would eventually leave Russia and arrived in Carmel sometime in the mid-1880s.

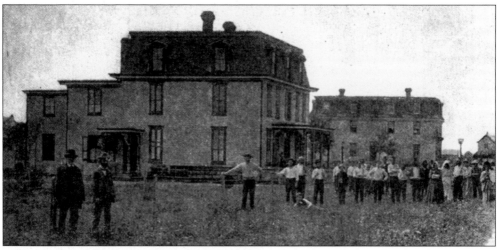

In an area three miles south of Rosenhayn, in a place called Beaver Dam, an entrepreneurial W. H. Miller, in an attempt to colonize, allowed some German immigrant families from Philadelphia to settle on his land. However, when the early families left to go back to Philadelphia, his plan almost died, until Michael Heilprin, who saw an opportunity there for his persecuted Jewish brethren, rescued the plan of colonization and created the colony of Carmel. This photograph is of Miller's residence, which also served as the colony's post office and library.

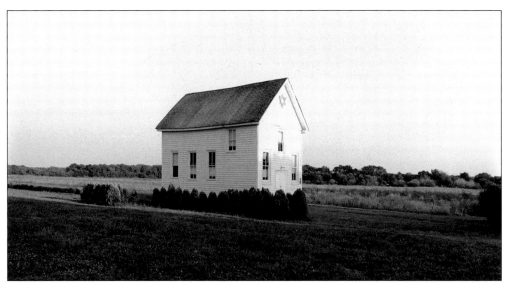

The last synagogue built in the 19th century in New Jersey was constructed in Rosenhayn, a Jewish farm colony/township in Cumberland County; built about 1898 by congregation Or Yisrael, it is located miles away from any population center. The location caused many to wonder how the early settlers got to services since the Orthodox sects are not permitted to ride on the Sabbath. Although well maintained, the synagogue does not appear to be in use. The synagogue was also known by the name Beth Israel Synagogue.

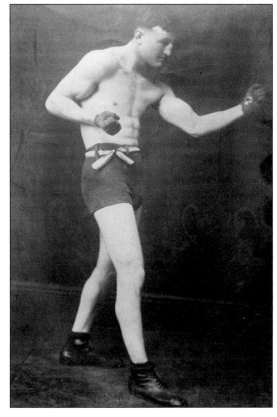

Born and raised in the Jewish farm colony of Rosenhayn, Alexander Rudolph would change his name to Al McCoy. On April 7, 1914, he became the first Jewish middleweight boxing champion. In the early 1900s, Jewish fighters would take on Irish names to capitalize on the popularity of Irish fighters. Other stories indicate that he changed his name in an effort to conceal his career from his parents. He turned professional at the age of 14, the third-youngest professional debut in boxing history.

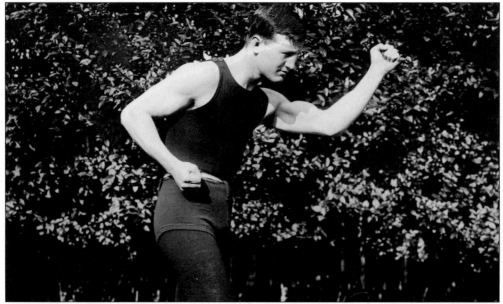

Al McCoy flattened champion George Chip in the first round of their title bout on April 7, 1914, to win the middleweight crown, this in an era when a champion could only lose his title by a knockout. McCoy battled through 46 fights, losing the middleweight title on November 14, 1917, on a sixth-round knockout by Mike O'Dowd. McCoy retired in 1920, having won 99 of 139 career decisions.

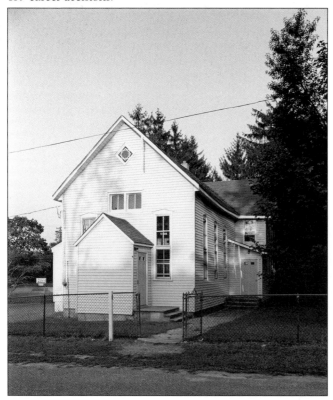

Organized in 1906 in the Jewish farm colony of Norma (some sources list the formation as early as 1888) with 26 charter members, Ahavas Achim was established as a rival to Vineland's Congregation Sons of Jacob. The group immediately began operating a Hebrew school in an old building on Plum Street. By the end of the year, the congregation had completed a new building an a *mikvah* (ritual bathhouse). Showing a lack of knowledge in Jewish tradition, a local newspaper described the building as a "commodious looking church with attached Turkish bathhouse or swimming pool." Looking at this building from the outside, there is no sign that suggests this is a house of worship.

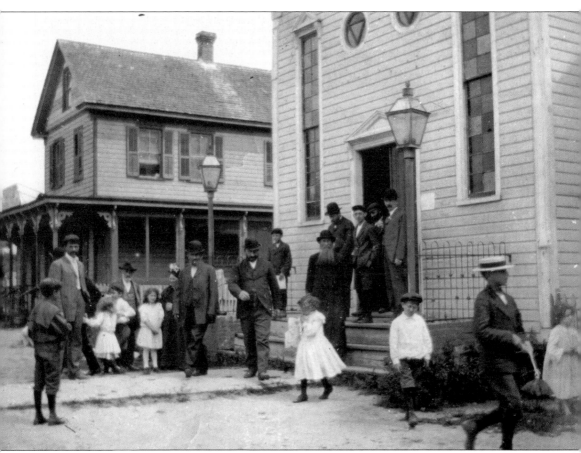

In this 1910 photograph are the residents of Norma leaving services from Ahavas Achim Congregation, possibly on a High Holiday.

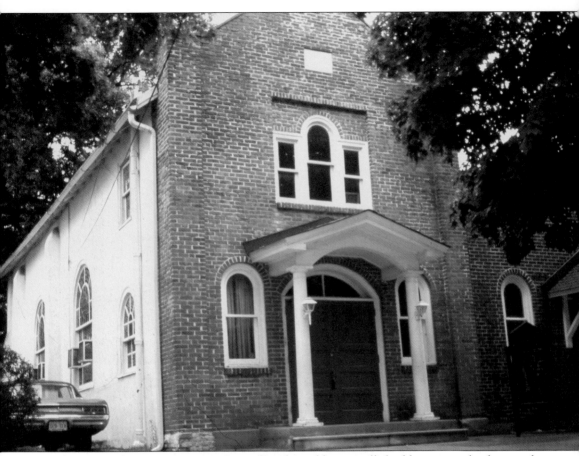

Not to be outdone, Congregation Sons of Jacob would eventually build its own mikvah, or as the local newspaper described it, "a Turkish bath and baptismal pool in the rear of their church."

Congregation Beth Abraham began in the late 1800s with services being held on the third floor of the Horner Building in Bridgeton. The total Jewish population of Bridgeton was about 30 families. The congregation would eventually move to hold services above the Cohen Cigar business on North Laurel Street. On June 26, 1915, a cornerstone was laid at the North Laurel Street site, which in 1916 became the permanent home of the synagogue.

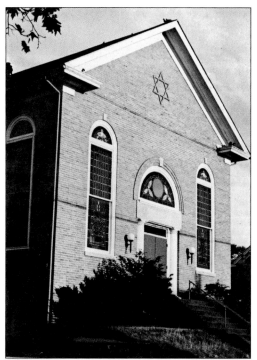

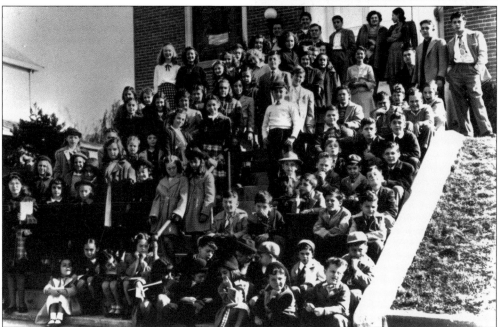

In 1942, the sanctuary was completely remodeled and a new altar was dedicated. At about the same time, the need for a religious school became apparent, as noted by the large student population seen in this photograph. At this time, congregation member Max Feinstein purchased the nearby Pritchard Canning Company for the building of the new facility. On May 23, 1953, the Harold S. Feinstein Memorial School of Congregation Beth Abraham, in honor of his deceased son, was officially dedicated.

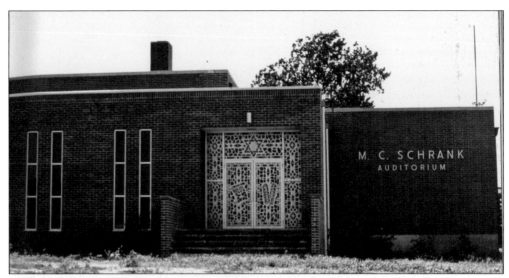

After a successful fund-raising effort in 1955, the second phase of the building process was begun. In 1958, the Max C. Schrank Auditorium was completed. By 1962, the old sanctuary was sold and construction began on a new synagogue, with groundbreaking taking place on Purim, March 22, 1970. The completed synagogue and auditorium is seen above in this 1971 image from the dedication ceremony. Unfortunately, because of the dwindling Jewish population, the building may soon go up for sale.

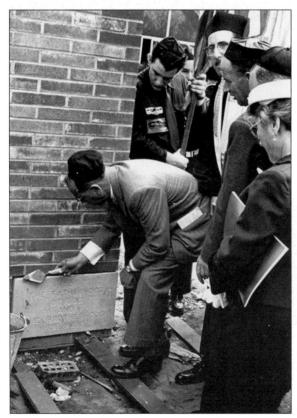

Members of Congregation Beth Israel of Vineland are at the laying of the cornerstone.

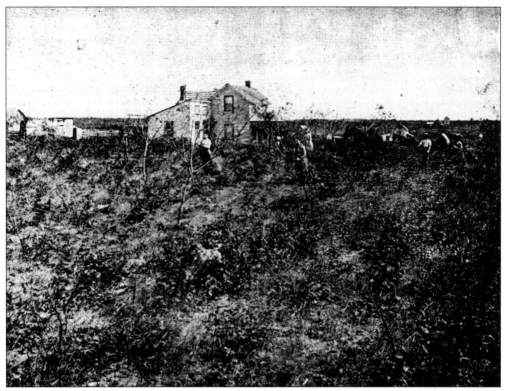

This photograph shows the homestead of a Mr. Josium, one of the original settlers of Rosenhayn.

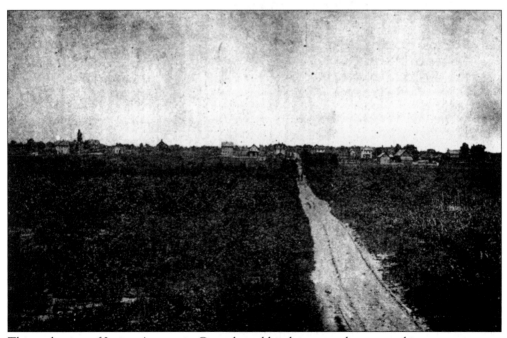

This early view of Irving Avenue in Carmel would in later years be surveyed into streets, many of which were named after the early pioneers of the colonies.

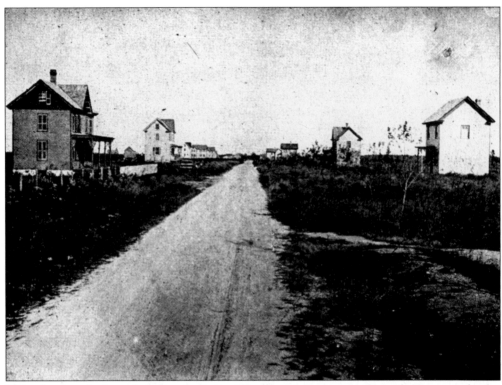

This photograph shows homesteads lining West Irving Avenue in Carmel. Homesteads also lined East Irving Avenue.

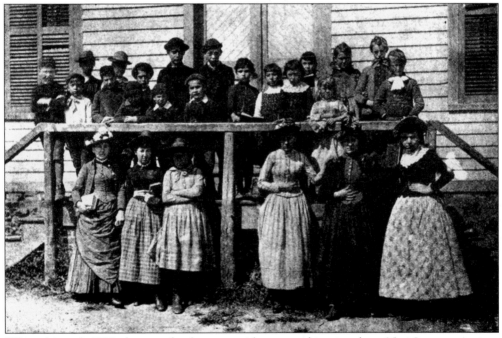

When this early-1900 photograph of teenage girls appeared in a southern New Jersey magazine, the caption read, "Young Jewish Element at Rosenhayn."

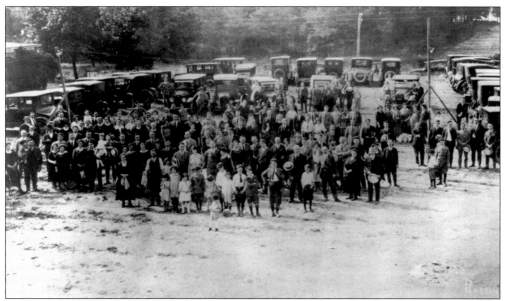

This 1923 image shows the annual Beth Israel (Vineland) congregational picnic at Rainbow Lake.

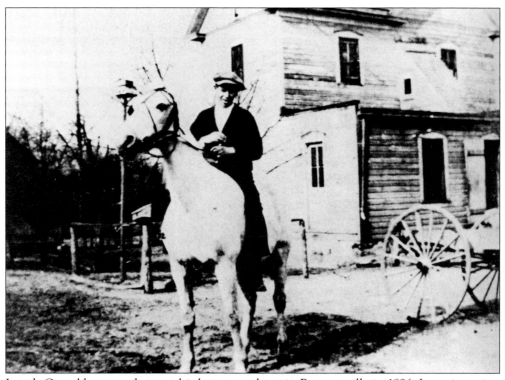

Joseph Greenblatt, seen here on his horse, was born in Brotmanville in 1896. In an interview before his death, he recalled that while growing up in Brotmanville, Yiddish was the primary language. According to one author of the histories of the Jewish farming communities, Greenblatt stated that it was "as if they took a village from Poland and brought it right here to Brotmanville."

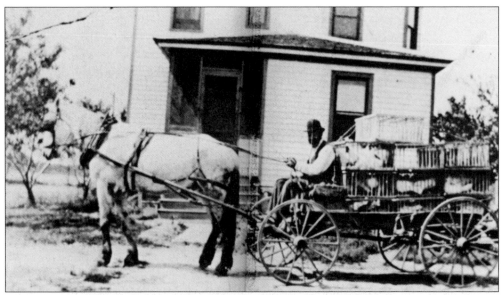

New Jersey would become one of the leading poultry and egg producing states in America, becoming known as the egg basket of America and as the cradle of the Jewish farm movement. Here Joseph Greenblatt is seen with his chicken wagon.

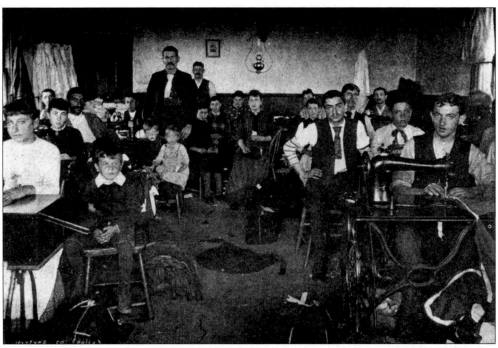

In this photograph, tailors are working at Castle Garden in Rosenhayn. The building was previously a cigar factory. Of interest are all the young children in the photograph; in all probability they were not just there because there was no one to mind them at home but instead were in the poorly ventilated work houses assisting their parents. This was an era when child labor laws did not exist or were poorly enforced.

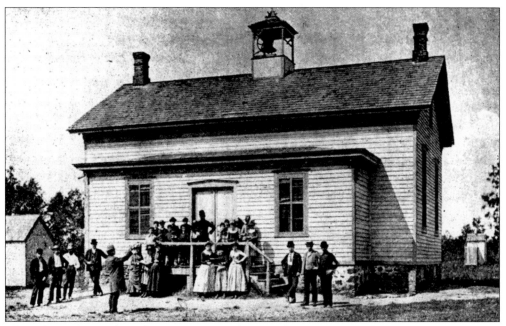

The colony of Rosenhayn began in 1882 with six Russian Jewish families; as it grew so did the need for a building to educate the children. Here the faculty and students are getting ready for a group picture in front of the schoolhouse at Rosenhayn.

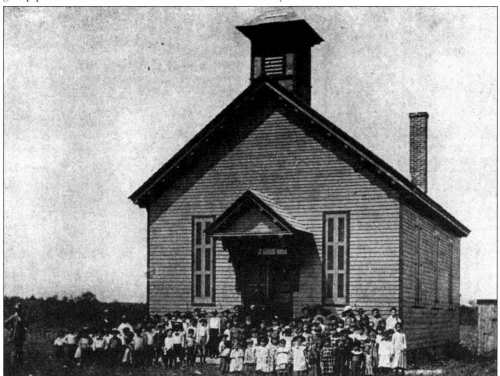

A group of children pose in front of the schoolhouse in Carmel. Like the parents of the other Jewish farm colonies, education was a priority for parents in Carmel.

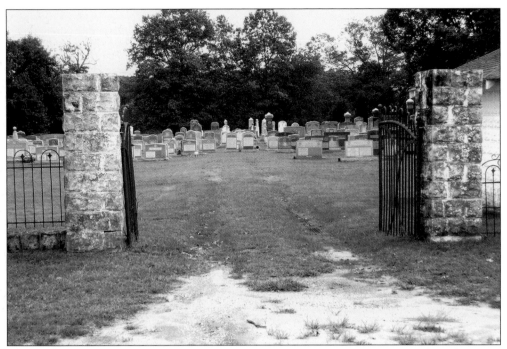

The Beth Abraham/Rosenhayn Jewish Cemetery became the final resting place for many original Jewish colonists. The community included the Garton Road settlement and later the Jews of Bridgeton in the county seat of Cumberland County.

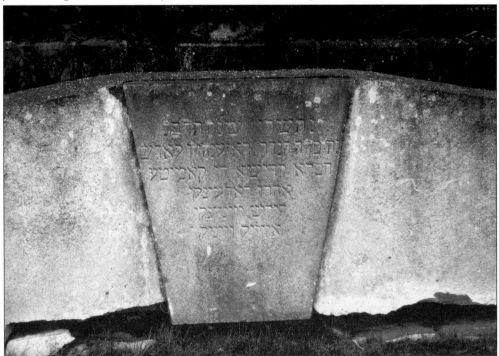

This photograph shows the archway that once appeared over the entrance of the Beth Abraham/Rosenhayn Jewish Cemetery.

Three

CAMDEN AND BURLINGTON COUNTIES

Although this chapter deals with the county of Camden, one cannot help, when discussing the Jewish history of the county, but concentrate on the city of Camden itself.

While African American and Hispanic families have given the city much of its recent flavor, as recently as the 1960s, about 10,000 Jews lived in Camden. They achieved prominence in all facets of the city's life, business, legal, political, and social sectors. Broadway, Federal Street, and especially Kaighn Avenue were the home of many Jewish-owned businesses.

The former Congregation Beth El's once lovely synagogue was razed, and a new Boys and Girls Club was erected in its place. The building was constructed with funds donated by Parkside native and professional sports team owner Lewis Katz.

Although Parkside is remembered as Camden's Jewish neighborhood, in reality Parkside was one of Camden County's first ethnically diverse neighborhoods. By 1915, it was home to every ethnic group, with the exception of African Americans, who remained in the Kaighnton and Centerville neighborhoods.

East Camden was the home of many Jewish businessmen and businesses, the best remembered probably being Kotlikoff's Department Store on Federal Street, while East Camden's Temple Beth Israel was the last new synagogue built in Camden.

A number of Jewish immigrants rose to prominence within Camden and a great many gave back in the form of monetary contributions to help build synagogues or in the form of advice, such as lawyers helping neighbors with legal problems, the doctor who would refuse a fee knowing a family did not have the money, or the local butcher or grocer who would run a tab until the next payday. This chapter looks at some of these people and the contributions they made not only to a thriving Jewish community but to the city as a whole.

In the 1960s, the Jewish community of the city migrated to other areas in the county such as Cherry Hill, where a number of the Camden County's synagogues were built and many of its Jewish community reside today. Those shall be examined here as well.

The city of Camden now counts less than 80,000 residents. Among these are an estimated 50 Jewish families.

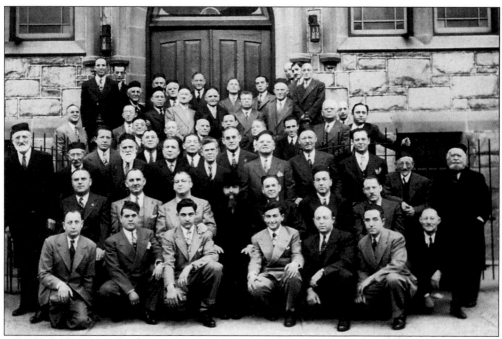

This 1944 image shows Rabbi Naftali Riff's Bible class gathered on the front steps of the Congregation Sons of Israel on South Eighth Street. Congregation Sons of Israel was the first synagogue in Camden, founded in 1894 by Rabbi David Shane, who served as the spiritual leader until 1917 when the position was taken over by Riff.

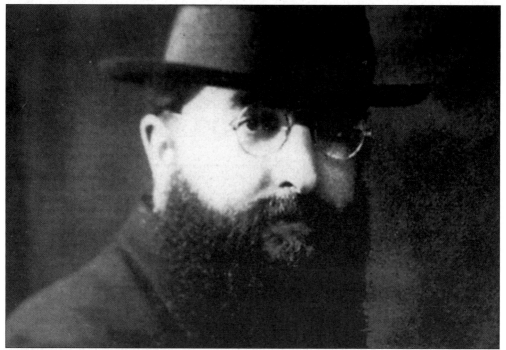

Riff was a highly revered spiritual leader of Congregation Sons of Israel, which was located at 1128 South Eighth Street, on the corner of South Eighth and Sycamore Streets.

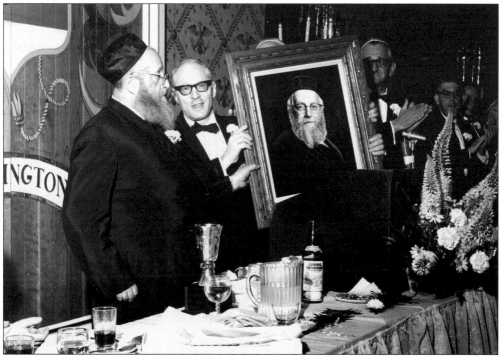

An Orthodox synagogue, Sons of Israel was popularly known in Camden's Jewish community as the "Eighth Street Schul." Riff led Sons of Israel from the early 1920s through the late 1960s.

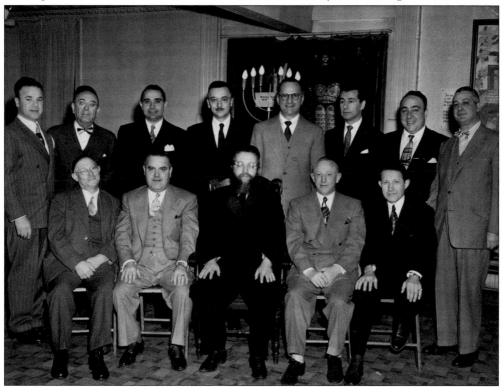

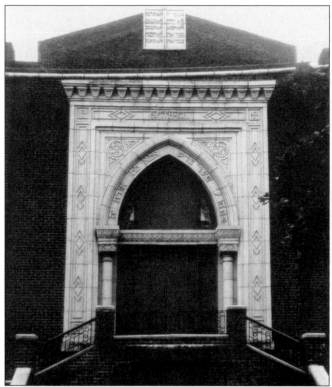

Congregation Beth El was Camden's first Conservative synagogue, representing one of American Judaism's three main branches. The congregation built and occupied a synagogue and school building on Park Boulevard, opposite Farnham Park, after World War I. It would occupy this structure until 1968, when the new building on Chapel Avenue in Cherry Hill was occupied.

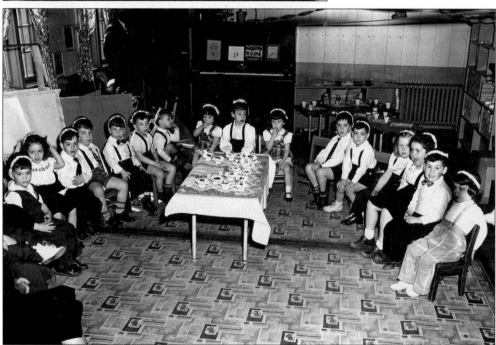

Rabbi Furman, a Holocaust survivor, was the principal of both the day school, which was known as the Beth El Academy, and of the afternoon religious school, which was in session on Sunday mornings and Tuesday and Thursday afternoons from 4:00 p.m. to 6:15 p.m.

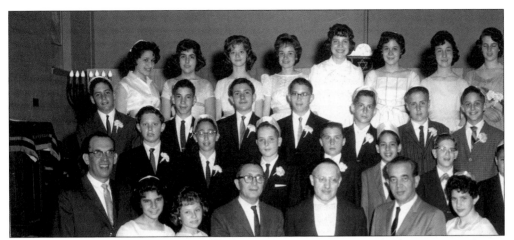

This photograph shows the graduating class of the Congregation Beth El synagogue when it was located in East Camden in 1960. Rabbi Max Weine is in the center of the photograph, and Cantor Kreigsman is on the right.

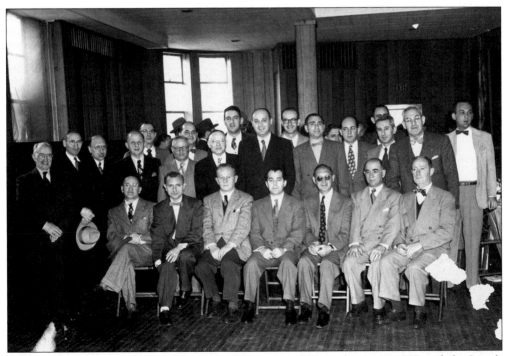

Rabbi Harry Kellman graduated from the University of Pennsylvania in 1927 and the Jewish Theological Seminary in 1931. Following his service as an army chaplain in World War II, he became rabbi at Beth Israel in Vineland for 17 years. Kellman developed a reputation as an "orator of note." He and his wife, Ruth, and their eight-year-old daughter, Nadine, moved to Camden, and he was installed as Beth El's rabbi on September 9, 1947. Kellman is seen in this image seated fourth from right at the Congregation Beth El synagogue rabbi's dinner.

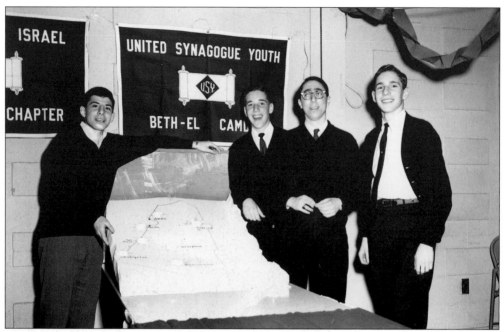

The synagogue and school building on Park Boulevard, opposite Farnham Park, boasted a very active youth group. Here members of the local Beth El chapter of the United Synagogue Youth proudly display their banner.

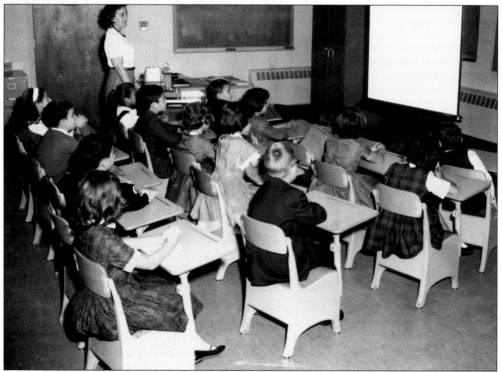

Temple Emanuel was a Reform congregation. This photograph shows a Hebrew school class at Temple Emanuel in October 1961.

Founded in February 1950, Temple Emanuel was the first Reform congregation in Cherry Hill. This 1957 groundbreaking photograph is of the construction of the synagogue at its Cooper River Parkway location.

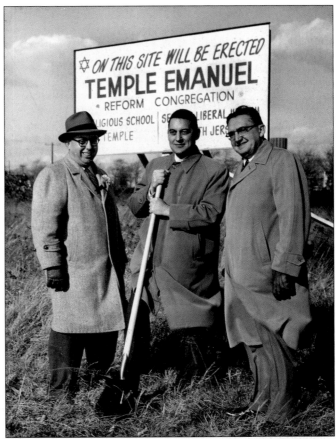

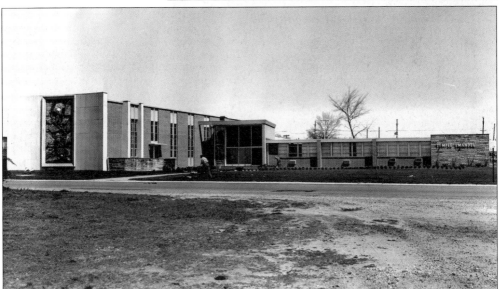

The Cooper River Parkway location of Temple Emanuel was occupied from 1959 through 1992, when the congregation relocated to its present location on Springdale and Kresson Roads in Cherry Hill.

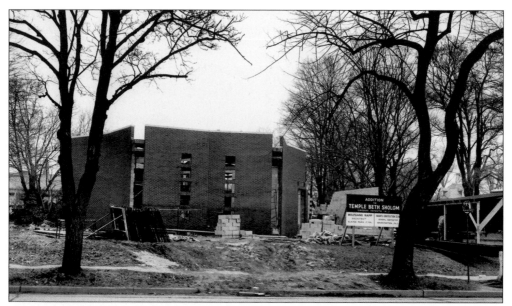

Temple Beth Shalom was founded over 50 years ago as Jews moved from Camden eastward. The first permanent location was in Haddon Heights. There it grew into a synagogue of over 600 families with a strong commitment to Jewish education and practices. This 1963 picture shows the construction of the addition, which was required because of the increased membership. In 1989, the synagogue moved to its current location on Kresson and Cropwell Roads in Cherry Hill.

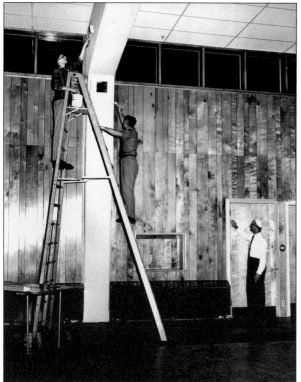

This June 1963 photograph is of the interior of Temple Beth Shalom during renovations for the new addition to the synagogue. Here contractors get some help from synagogue members Sol Wolden (left), Donald Kurtzman (center), and Edward Kurtzman.

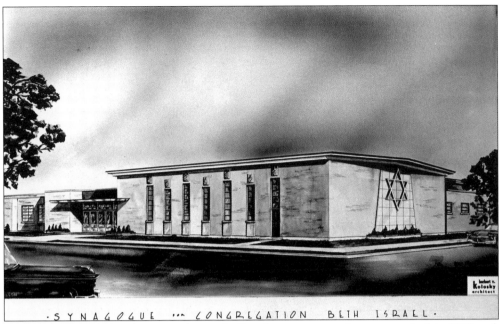

·SYNAGOGUE ··· CONGREGATION BETH ISRAEL·

Congregation Beth Israel was another early Camden synagogue. It was organized in 1929 and, according to Camden city historian Phil Cohen, was the first synagogue to be built in East Camden. By 1956, Congregation Beth Israel erected a new, modern synagogue at 315 Grand Avenue, just off Marlton Avenue.

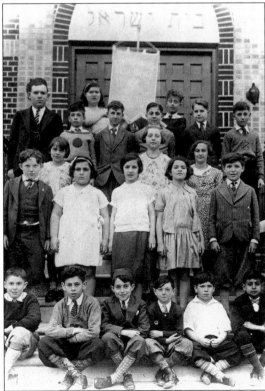

Between 1918 and 1924, the Jewish community of Camden built three new buildings. Two were synagogues, Sons of Israel at South Eighth and Sycamore Streets and Beth El on Park Boulevard at Belleview Avenue. The other building was the Talmud Torah School at 621 Kaighn Avenue. Built in 1924, the building later housed the Camden Jewish Center and the offices of the Jewish Federation. Here a group of children proudly displays its school banner in front of the Talmud Torah School.

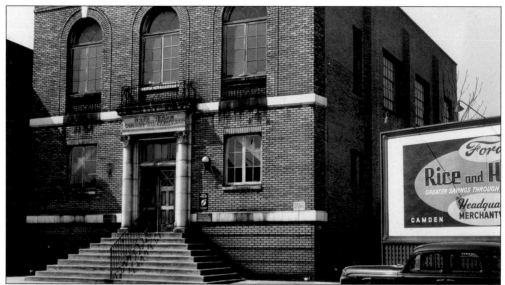

Built in 1924, the Talmud Torah building, located at 621 Kaighn Avenue, was established to ensure that the American-born children of Jewish immigrant parents would receive a good religious education. Many gifted teachers worked there over the years, including Ezekiel Jacob Levin, who taught there in 1926 and 1927. He would return to South Jersey in 1960 to become the director of the Bureau of Jewish Education of Camden, a position he held until his retirement in 1971. As the Jewish population of Camden began to move to the suburbs, the need for a building in Camden diminished. In 1966, the building became a Masonic center under the aegis of the Masonic Association of Camden.

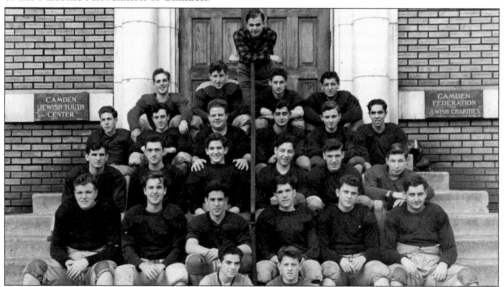

In the early years in Camden, the Talmud Torah building also served as the local Jewish Community Center (JCC) for the youth of the area. There were many athletic teams and other programs that were operated from the Camden JCC/Young Men's Hebrew Association (YMHA). Athletic teams, which included football as pictured here, were an important part of the many youth programs at the JCC. Note the sign on the Talmud Torah building: "Camden Jewish Youth Center."

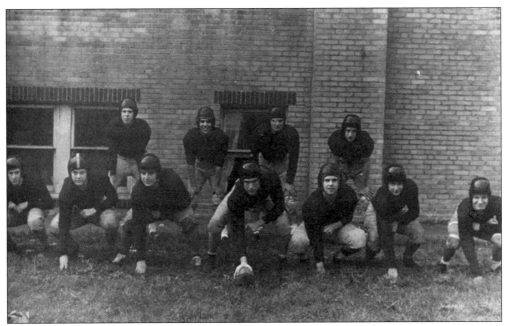

This is a photograph of the Camden Jewish Youth Center football team in full gear posing in front of the Talmud Torah building.

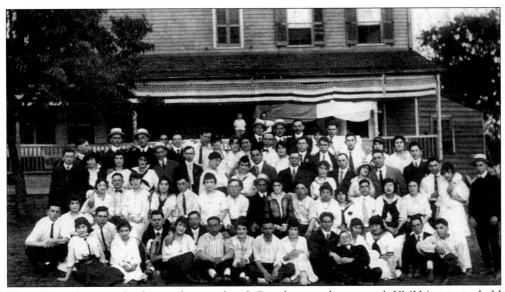

This 1916 photograph shows the youth of Camden at the annual YMHA picnic held in Blackwood.

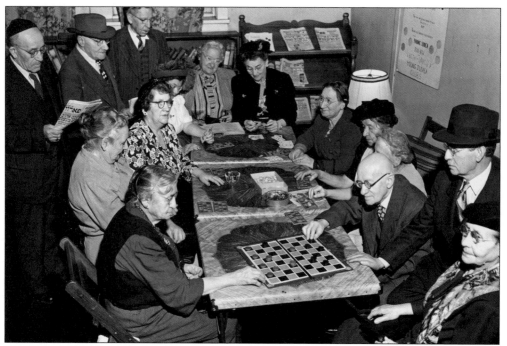

The Talmud Torah building was not just for the city's youth but for its seniors as well. Members of the Golden Club senior citizens organization, shortly after its founding, are seen meeting in the Talmud Torah building, which had formerly served as the area's JCC.

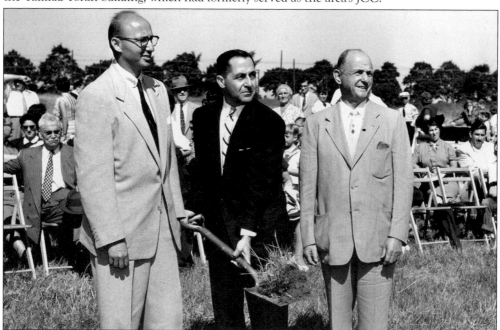

The Jewish community of the region continued to grow and with it so did the needs of the community. In 1953, a groundbreaking ceremony for a new JCC on Route 70 in Pennsauken was conducted. From left to right, Max Odlen, Judge William Lipkin, and Joseph Odlen perform the honors.

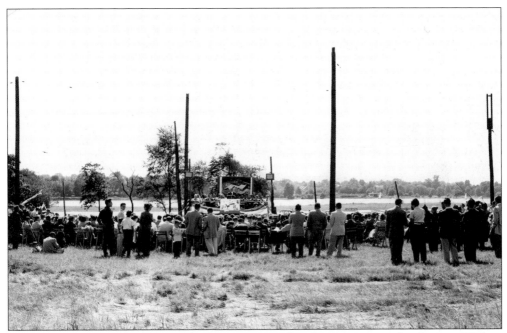

This 1953 image shows a large crowd at the groundbreaking ceremony for the new JCC in Pennsauken. Predecessor to today's JCC, the first YMHA and Young Women's Hebrew Association (YWHA) in Camden was located at 570–572 Walnut Street from 1917 to 1928. The building later became the Calvary Tabernacle in 1947.

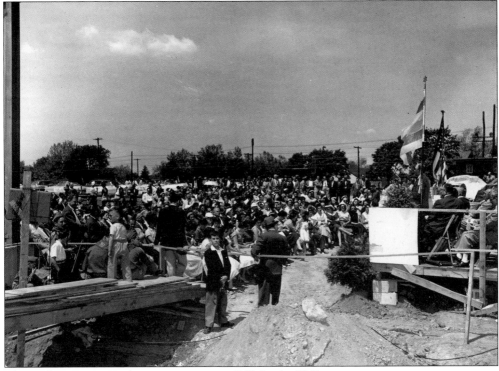

This is the cornerstone-laying ceremony in 1955 for the JCC.

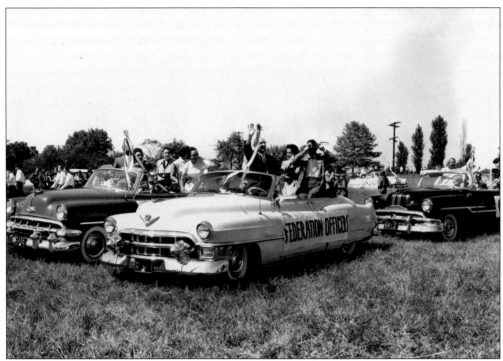

With the entire community celebrating, this convertible would lead the parade to the groundbreaking of the new JCC on Route 70 in Pennsauken in 1953.

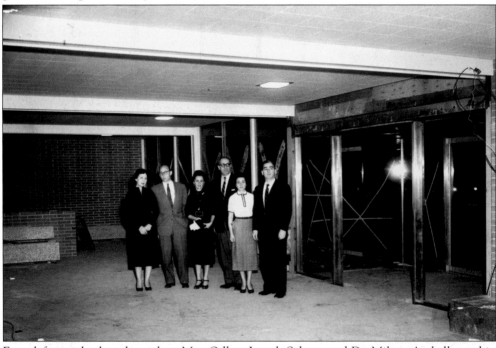

From left to right, board members Max Odlen, Joseph Schurr, and Dr. Milton Asebell stand in the front of an almost completed JCC on Marlton Pike (Route 70) in Pennsauken. The females in the photograph are not identified.

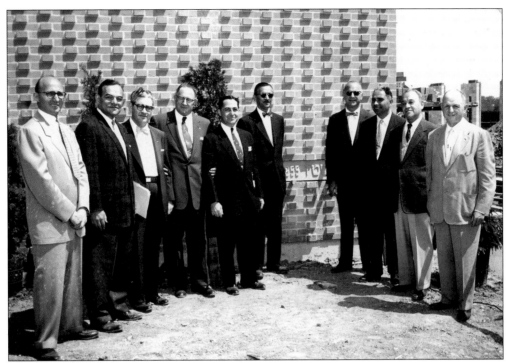

Leaders of the community, officers of the Jewish Federation, and leaders of the building fund are at the cornerstone-laying ceremony for the new JCC in 1955.

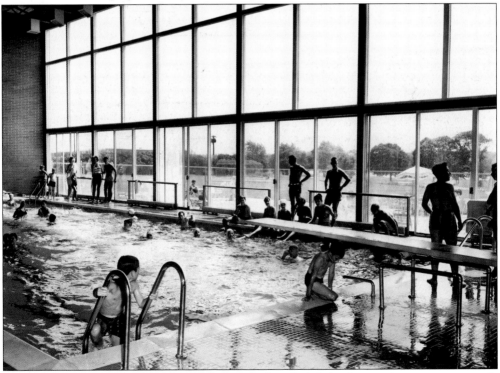

The new JCC would boast about its facilities, which included this large indoor swimming pool.

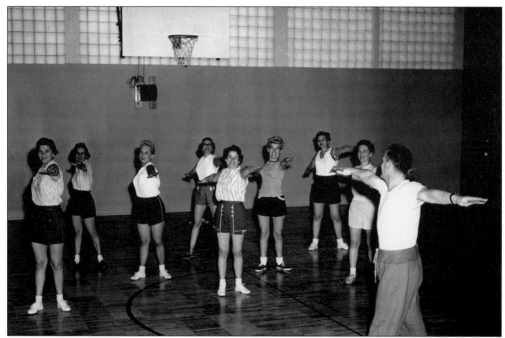

Physical fitness in the 1950s was not as popular as it is today; however, there was a trend beginning, and the JCC would help to take the lead for those who wished to participate.

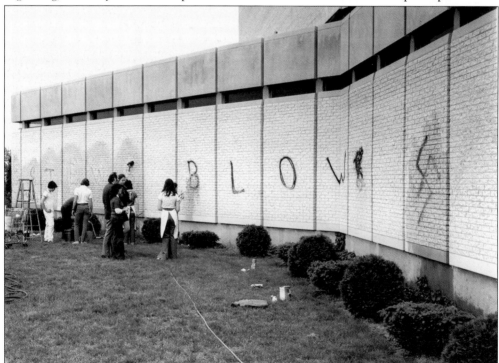

Anti-Semitism was never far away, as seen in this photograph. The outside of the JCC is spray painted with hate messages. The graffiti was painted over and cleaned up by the center's youth group.

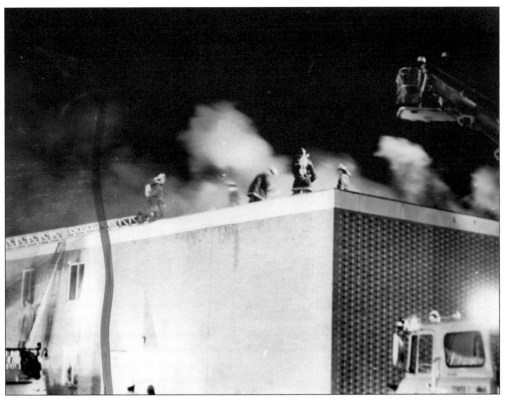
In the early 1970s, fire struck the JCC in Pennsauken, causing extensive damage to the facility.

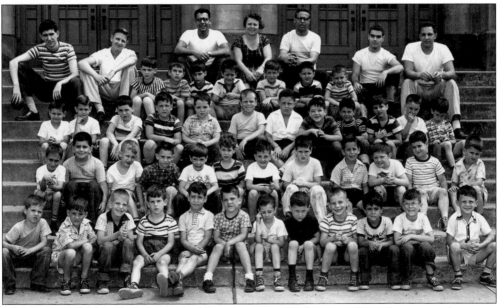
In May 1942, the Jewish Federation of Camden announced sponsorship of a summer day camp, the forerunner of Camp Hilltop. This summer day camp program operated from various locations in Camden, including the Talmud Torah as well as Camden High School, where this group of campers sits posing for a picture.

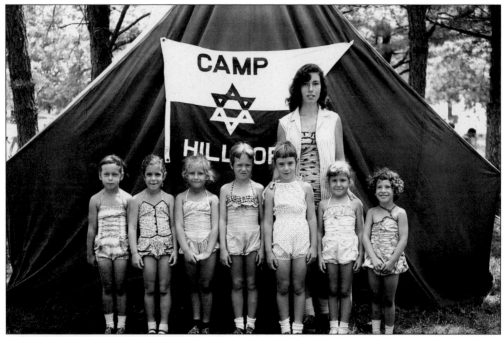

In May 1960, one of Congregation Beth El's most outstanding leaders passed away. The death of E. George Aaron was a severe blow, not only to the Jewish community but to all of Camden. His legacy would live on for future Jewish summer campers.

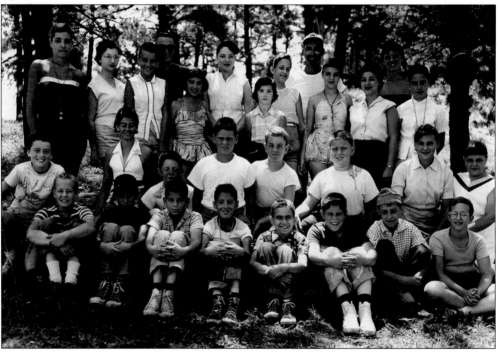

One of E. George Aaron's last magnanimous gestures was arranging for the sale of his 83-acre summer retreat at Medford to the JCC for use as Camp Hilltop, the summer day camp. The price was so low as to make the transaction almost an outright gift.

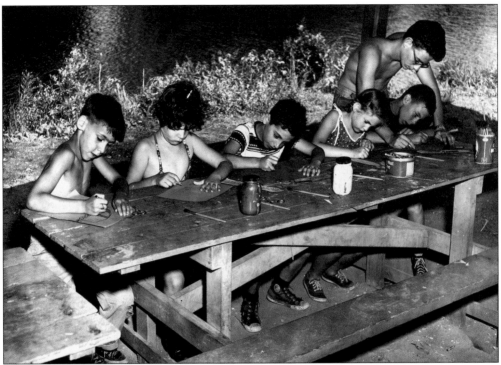

The tree-lined Medford campground offered a retreat from the hot city and allowed children to engage in supervised activities, such as these children working on their arts and crafts projects.

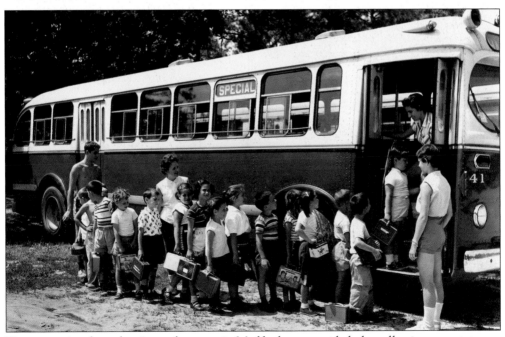

Transportation from the city to the camp in Medford was provided, thus allowing parents to use their own vehicles for work and to not have to worry about driving the children to camp, which was over 45 minutes away.

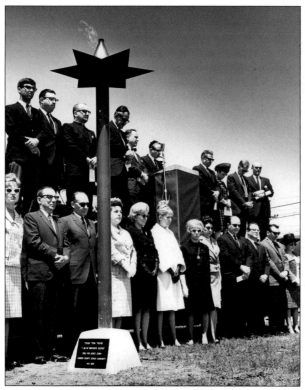

The Camden community was very active in the struggle for freeing Jews from the then Soviet Union. In this photograph, Robert Greenberg, representing the Jewish youth group; Rabbi Bernard Rothman of Congregation Sons of Israel; Joseph Lebow, the president of the Jewish Federation; Morton Jacobs, Esq., the chair of the Jewish Relations Council; and Rabbi Lester Hering of Congregation Beth Jacob show their solidarity with their oppressed Jewish brothers at a community vigil for Soviet Jewry in May 1966.

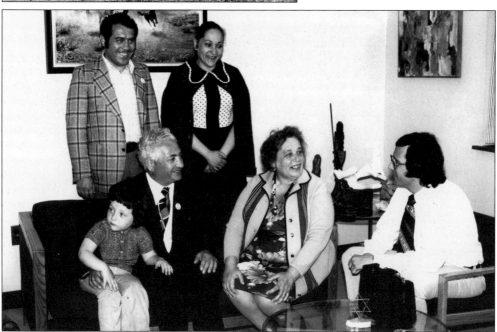

Because of pressures brought to bear on the Soviet Union by groups such as those in southern New Jersey, some Jews were eventually granted exit visas. These Jews would be sponsored by local families and set up in apartments and assisted with finding work. This newly arrived Soviet family gets introduced and welcomed by Joel Kaber (left).

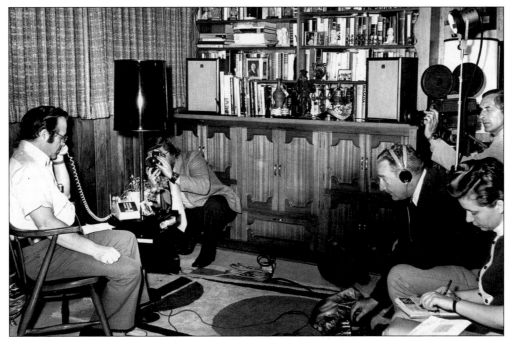

Constant encouragement was given to the Jews in the Soviet Union. In this telephone conversation with a Soviet Jewish leader in the USSR, assurance and encouragement are being given by a local Jewish leader. The conversation was taped for later radio broadcast.

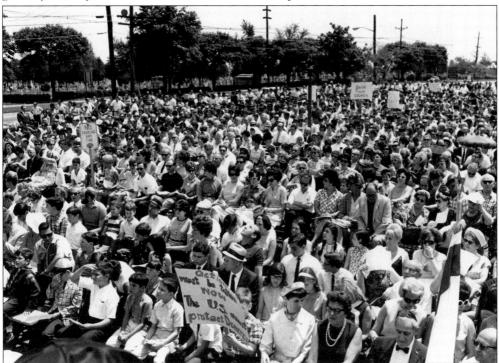

This large crowd at the JCC in Pennsauken is asking for the United States to help Israel. This, in all probability, was during the 1967 war.

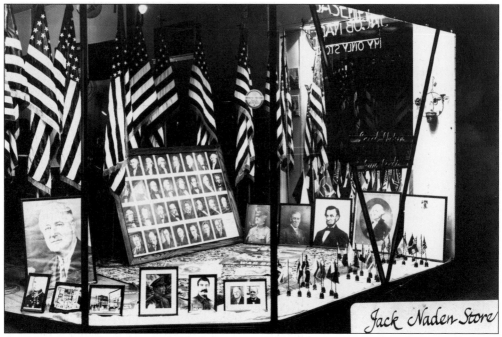

As this window display in Jack Naden's store in 1942 demonstrates, Jewish patriotism was evident in Camden. Of interest in this display is a picture of Joseph Stalin (foreground, center of window). This was at a time when the United States and Russia were allies.

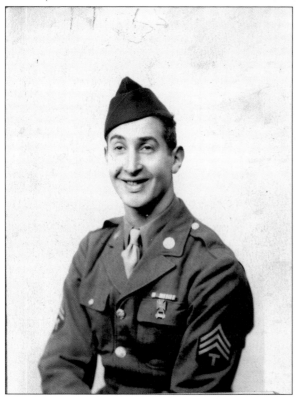

Camden resident Jack Minkoff, like many other Jewish residents of Camden, proudly served his country in World War II.

This 1946 photograph shows Camden resident Jay Richelson in uniform during World War II. On October 22, 1945, there was a memorial held for 22 Jewish servicemen from Camden who had died.

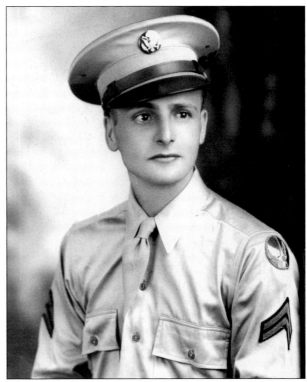

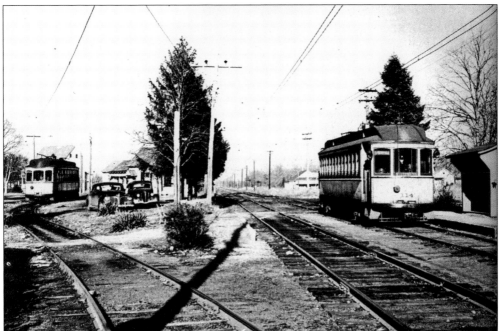

With the start of the Camden–Atlantic City Railroad, both Camden residents as well as those from across the river in Philadelphia could enjoy either day trips or vacations lasting a few days. Atlantic City would become South Jersey's playground for the Jews of Camden and Philadelphia.

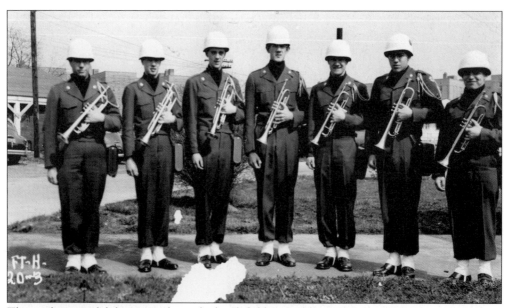

Those who served did so not only on the battlefield, some like Camden resident Dave Zuckerberg (far left) served by helping to boost moral. Zuckerberg was stationed at Fort Hamilton as part of the 325th Army Band.

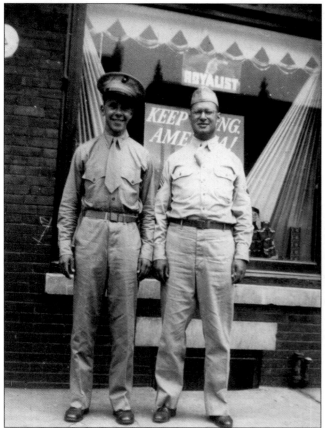

Brothers Lamar (left) and Norris Spewak are seen here posing in uniform during World War II. Lamar became known locally as Jack Lamar, the longtime and well-known voice of Keystone Race Track, now Philadelphia Park. He also called races at Garden State Park in Cherry Hill. He is recalled fondly by race fans for his great voice and staccato call of a race. His calls went like this: It's Secretariat first, Seattle Slew second, Citation third, and so on. It did not matter if it was the lowest maiden claimer or a stakes, it was always the same call. Lamar died on April 8, 2006.

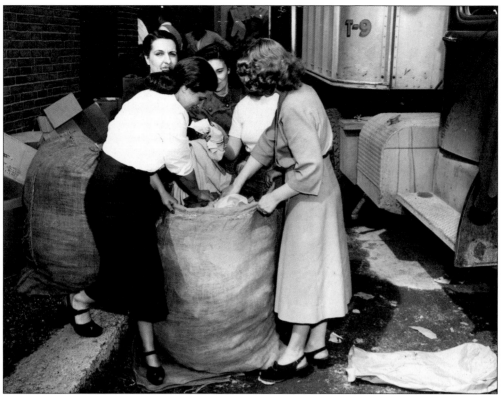

Here Camden residents Ann Lemerman (left foreground) and Ruth Goodman (right foreground) pack relief supplies as part of a drive to assist victims and refugees in war-ravaged Europe shortly after World War II ended.

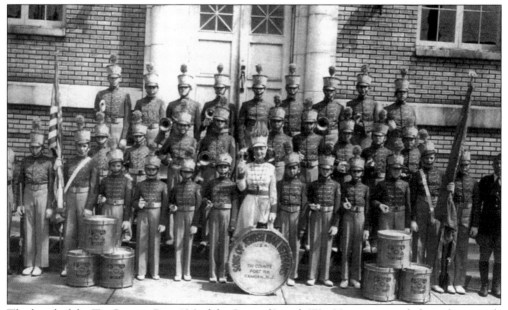

The band of the Tri-County Post 126 of the Sons of Jewish War Veterans stands for a photograph before marching off in a Camden parade.

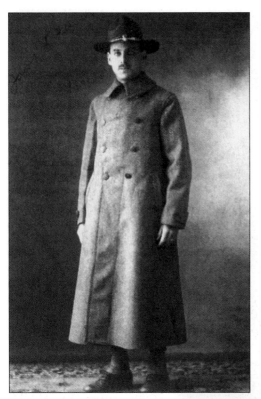

Jacob L. Furer, a Camden resident, is seen here in his World War I uniform. Furer became a prominent lawyer as well as a community leader after the war. In 1928–1929, he served as president of the Camden YMHA. The Camden Jewish War Veterans post, which now meets in Cherry Hill, is named after him.

This photograph shows Jacob L. Furer presenting a service flag to Carleton R. Hopkins, principal of Camden High School. The presentation was made on behalf of Tri-County Post 126 of the Jewish War Veterans on December 7, 1945. Furer also served as one of the early presidents of the Camden JCC.

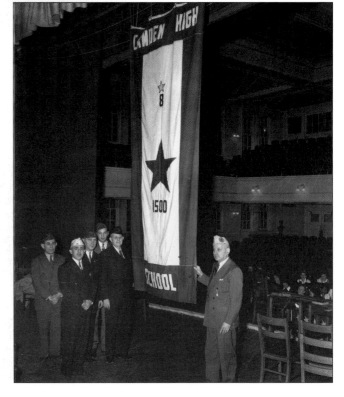

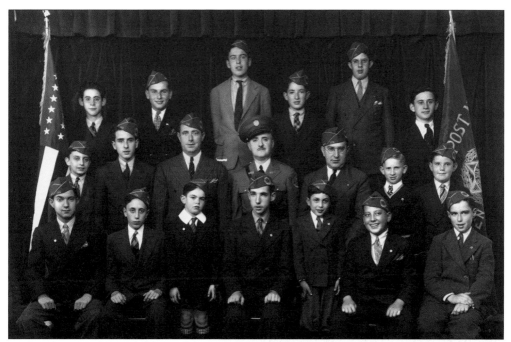

In this photograph are children of the Jewish War Veterans from Tri-County Post 126.

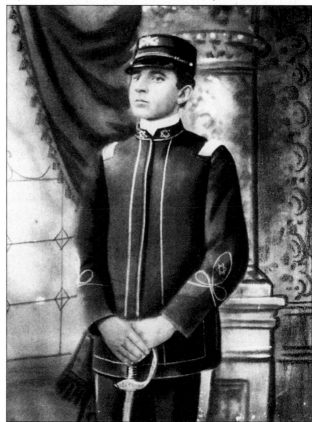

Louis Blum of Camden fought in the Spanish-American War. This photograph is from 1898. Of interest are the sleeves of the uniform, which bear a Star of David.

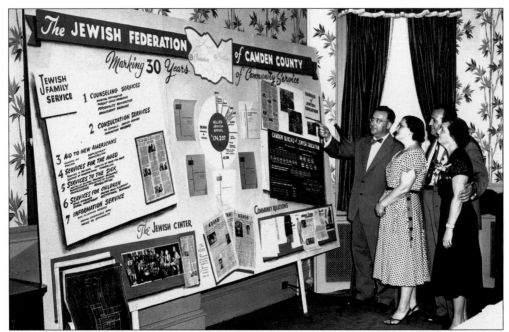

This photograph shows the celebration of the 30th year of the Jewish Federation of Camden County. Founded by a group of 29 men and women to serve and assist Jews in the city of Camden, it was originally known as the Federation of Jewish Charities and would later become known as the Jewish Federation of Southern New Jersey. The federation and its agencies provide services in the areas of social welfare, recreation, acculturation, and aid to new Americans, as well as counseling, advocacy, educational and cultural programs, and services for the aged.

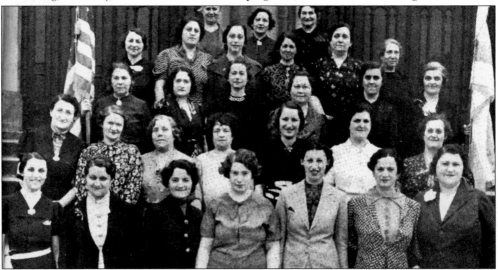

Founded in 1843, B'nai B'rith International is one of the world's largest and oldest Jewish human rights, community action, and humanitarian organizations. B'nai B'rith has founded hospitals, orphanages, senior housing communities, disaster relief campaigns, and libraries, as well as anti-hatred programs. B'nai B'rith is also a tireless advocate for Israel and the Diaspora in a variety of governmental and political arenas. In this 1937 photograph, the B'nai B'rith Women's Auxiliary of Camden is seen.

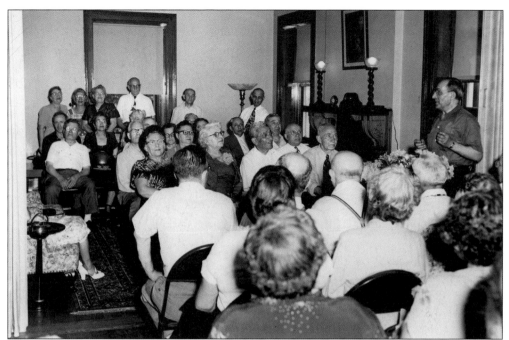

Created a century ago in 1906 by immigrants as a mutual aid society, the organization known as the Workman's Circle became known for building bonds of support and community. Branches formed across North America, providing communities of fellowship and a visionary safety net of health and education services, aiding Jewish families throughout the life cycle. Here a c. 1950 Workman's Circle meeting is taking place with Camden resident Joseph Epstein presiding.

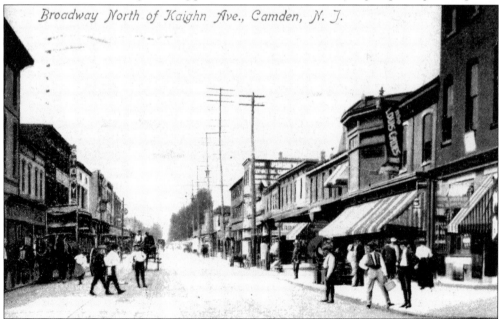

Broadway North of Kaighn Ave., Camden, N. J.

Harry Pinsky came to the United States from Russia in the late 1880s. He opened up a furniture store in Camden in 1891, which his son Reuben took charge of in 1906. A sign advertising the store can be seen in this late-1890s image.

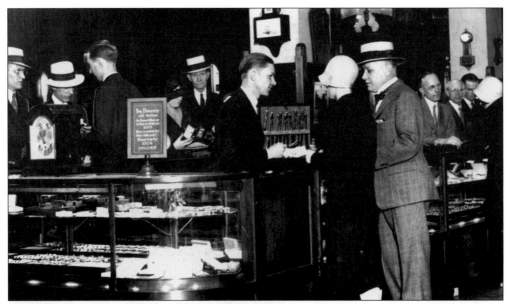

The Pinsky business grew to the point that it required a five-story building at the corner of Broadway and Spruce Street, which opened in 1924. Here opening day shoppers are dressed in their finest to look over the merchandise. By 1936, the Pinsky store moved to 921 Broadway. The Pinsky building was acquired by a furniture business called Whitehill, which operated at the location through the late 1940s. This building was later acquired by Joseph DiMona Sr. The Pinsky store would move one more time, to 941 Broadway. The business had closed by 1950.

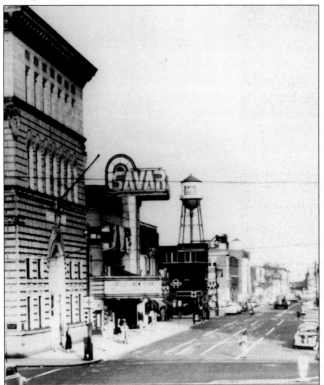

The Savar was the flagship theater of the Savar Theatre Corporation chain, which was founded by Samuel Varbalow. His brother Joseph A. Varbalow also served as an officer of the corporation, as well as practicing law in Camden. Another brother, Harry, passed away in 1940. Other theaters in the Savar chain in Camden included the Auditorium (which was torn down and rebuilt as the Rio), the Victoria, the Towers, the Midway, and the Arlo.

Seidman's hardware store in 1918 is seen here. Store clerk Harry Screibstein is on the far left. He was the father of Tri-County Jewish Historical Society director Ruth Bogutz.

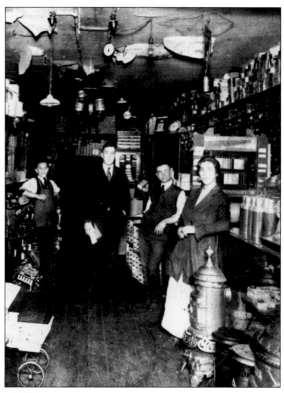

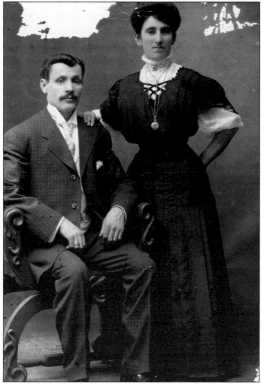

Two of Camden's early residents were Joseph and Yetta Plotnick, seen here in their May 17, 1907, wedding picture taken in Camden.

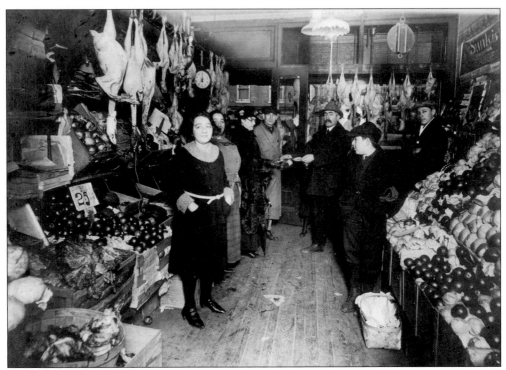

These pictures, taken around 1926, show Samuel Asbell's Fruit Market, which was located at 1146 Broadway. One can see the wide selection of products available, including the geese so prominently displayed throughout the store. The store also offered a large selection of fresh fruits and vegetables.

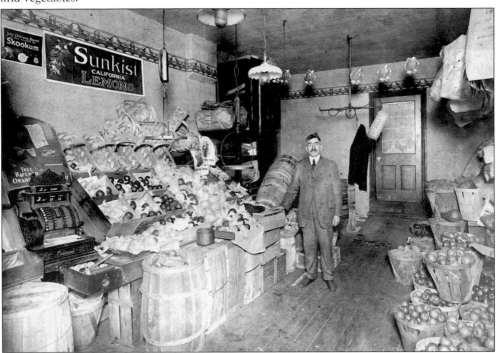

Rabbi Louis Segal, with his wife, Esther, sons, Sam and Nathan, and daughter, Sadie, poses in this 1910 portrait. Segal was one of the early rabbis to serve in a synagogue in Camden. Most synagogues operated without a rabbi until the influx from Europe brought a large number of trained rabbis to the United States. Segal served as the rabbi of the Liberty Street synagogue from 1910 to 1925.

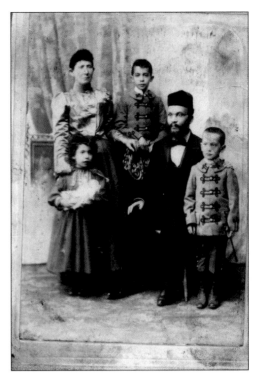

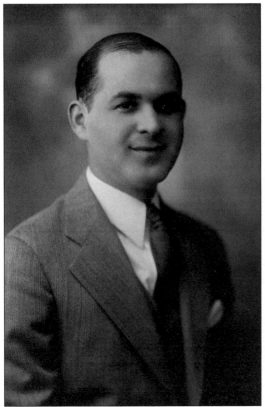

Mary Naden and her family operated a furniture and home furnishings business on Kaighn Avenue at Clover Street in Camden for the better part of five decades. One son, Jacob Naden (pictured), also operated a second shop in East Camden on Federal Street at Twenty-fourth Street in the 1930s and 1940s. Interestingly, the local newspaper the *Courier-Post* reported on February 10, 1936, that Jacob Naden acquired the "northwest corner Twenty-fourth and Federal Streets, north side Federal Street, 20 feet west Twenty-fourth Street" from "Velma E. Duncan et al" for only $1, a bargain even in that era.

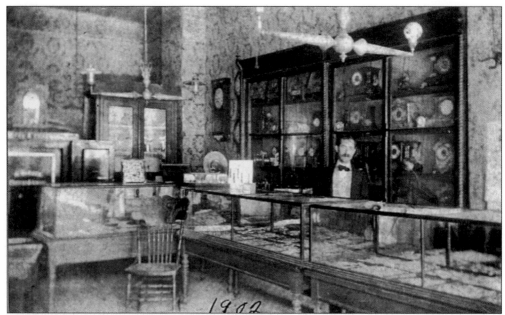

Nurock Jewelry Store was located at 1124 Broadway in Camden. The photograph above was taken in 1902 and shows lighting fixtures that were equipped for both gas and electric use. Electricity was still considered too unreliable an energy source to be relied on solely. The picture below shows the interior of the store a few years later; note that the lighting has been replaced and is now entirely electric.

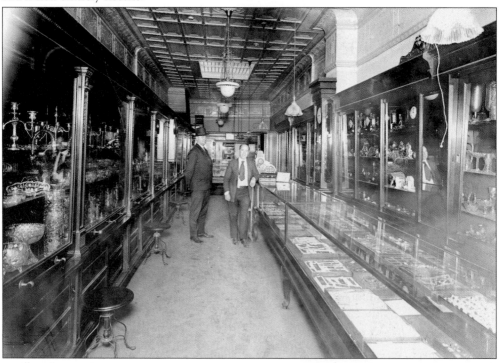

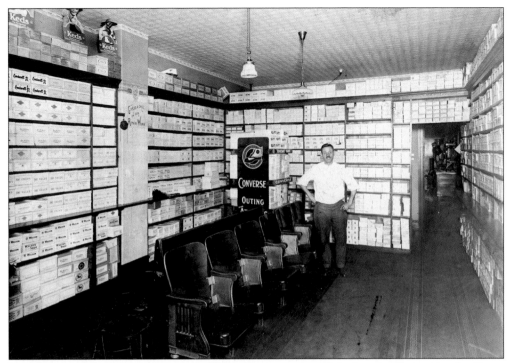

Founded in 1931, Shapiro Corrective Shoe Store was started during the Depression by Harry and Roslyn Shapiro. The store was located at 219 Broadway and was well known by podiatrists in the surrounding communities as the place to refer patients who required corrective footwear. The store closed in the 1960s.

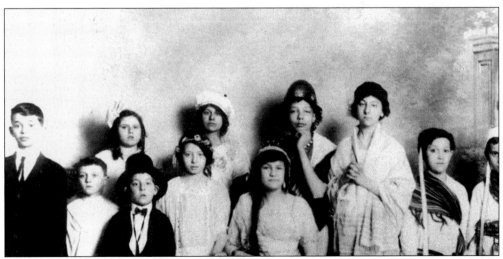

This photograph, taken in 1913 at an unknown Burlington County synagogue, shows children dressed in traditional Purim dress, probably during a Purim party or play. Marybelle Ellis is playing Queen Ester while Lillian Kaplan is playing the part of Hyman.

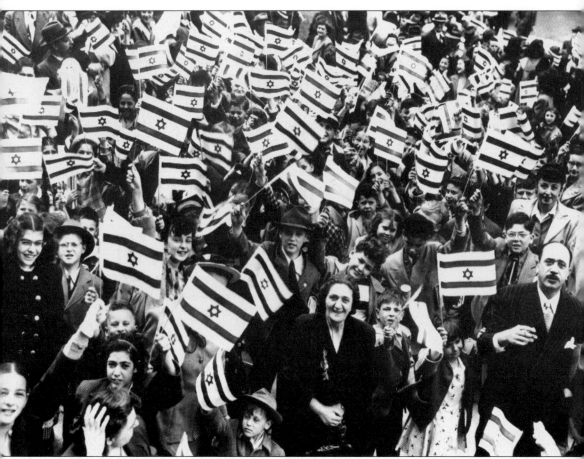

This May 16, 1948, picture shows Camden children waving new Israeli flags celebrating the establishment of the Israeli statehood. Children from all parts of Camden were on hand during the mass meeting and parade organized by the Camden Jewish War Veterans.

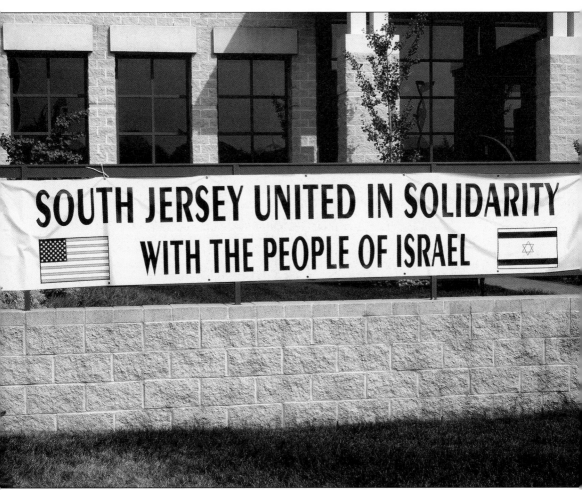

This sign is displayed outside the Katz Jewish Community Center in Cherry Hill. It was displayed in support of Israel during its war with the Hezbollah guerrilla fighters in Lebanon in July and August 2006.

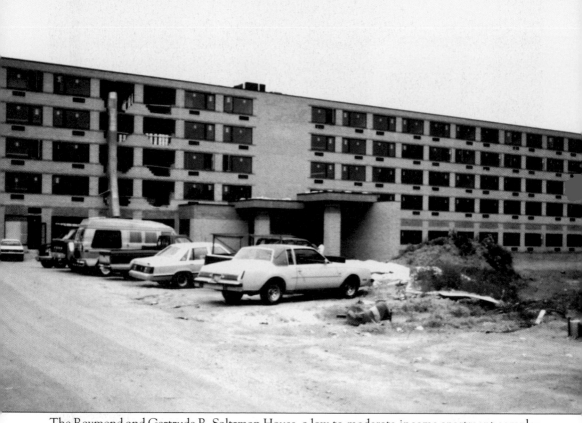

The Raymond and Gertrude R. Saltzman House, a low-to-moderate-income apartment complex, provides independent and assisted living facilities for the elderly in the community. The complex is administered by the Jewish Federation of Southern New Jersey, which encompasses Camden, Burlington, and Gloucester Counties and is the third-largest federation in the state of New Jersey.

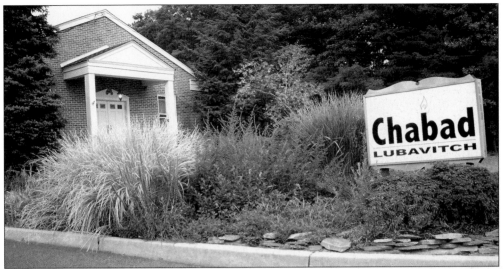

Chabad-Lubavitch is one of the largest branches of Hasidic Judaism and one of the largest Jewish Orthodox movements worldwide, especially in the United States and Israel. Chabad is a Hebrew acronym for "wisdom, understanding, knowledge." Lubavitch, taken from the Russian meaning "town of brotherly love," is the name of the town that served as the movement's headquarters for over a century. Today there are over 200,000 adherents to the movement. This Chabad-Lubavitch center is located in Cherry Hill.

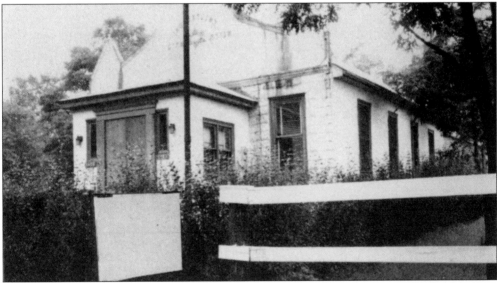

Just prior to World War I, a tract of land within Mount Laurel Township owned by Dr. Bruce was purchased by the Philadelphia Association of Realty and the Eagle Progress Association. The land was cut up into one-acre parcels, and 25 Russian immigrant families, who were unhappy with the slumlike conditions of nearby Philadelphia, were relocated to the property between Mount Laurel–Hainesport Road and Elbo Lane. Because the area was so open and clean, middle-class Jews from Camden and Philadelphia would use the area as a weekend getaway, and the name Springville was adopted; eventually the area would be known by the derogatory name of "Jewtown." The group built its own synagogue, Agudas Achim, which operated until the membership merged with Temple Sinai in Cinnaminson in 1971.

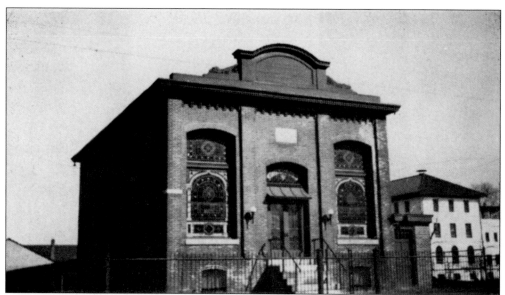

Gloucester City is a working class city in Camden County. Once lined with Jewish businesses, King Street was the heart of Gloucester City's Jewish community. Along with the many businesses on King Street was the Beth-El Congregation. Erected in 1887, the building first was a bank then the town's post office before being purchased and converted into a synagogue. The interior of the building was adorned with 12-foot-high stained-glass windows.

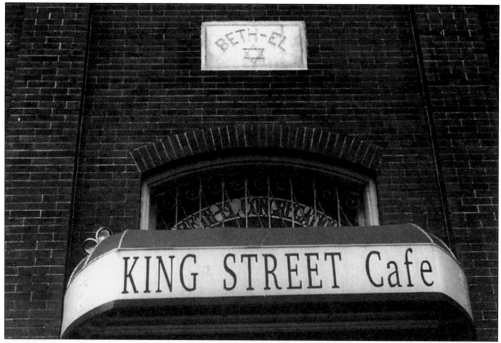

Like the Jewish community of Camden, the Jews of Gloucester City eventually migrated to the suburbs of Camden County, like Cherry Hill. The synagogue has since served as an artist studio and more recently, as seen in this 2002 photograph, as a café.

Four

MERCER AND
MONMOUTH COUNTIES

Although political correctness would today prevent it, in the 1920s and 1930s "All off for Jewtown" was a commonly heard phrase used by Irish bus and trolley drivers when approaching Trenton's Jewish neighborhood. Amazingly this was not considered offensive by a majority of the inhabitants of the neighborhood, who by 1860 numbered over 6,000, about the same as Presbyterians in the city but still far behind the city's 48,000 Catholics. Still by 1923 there were six synagogues in Trenton representing all three major branches.

Trenton's organized Jewish roots begin with the Har Sini Cemetery Association, which would purchase a plot of land at Vroom and Liberty Streets for the city's first Jewish cemetery. This group would evolve into Trenton's first synagogue Temple Har Sini, a Reform congregation. The earliest Orthodox congregation was Brothers of Israel, which was incorporated in 1883 and was lead by Rabbi Issachar Levin.

By 1904, Congregation Brothers of Israel erected the city's first Talmud Torah, which was named after the father of Zionism, Dr. Theodor Herzl. Trenton would soon become the center of Mercer County's Jewish population.

Jersey Homesteads, the subject of books, documentaries, and doctoral dissertations eventually becoming part of Monmouth County's Jewish history, is part of this book as well. Created during the Great Depression as part of Pres. Franklin Delano Roosevelt's New Deal, its post office address and telephone exchange were located in Hightstown, Mercer County. Sold in 1940, the town incorporated as a separate township from Hightstown and became part of Monmouth County.

The plan was to resettle Jewish garment workers from New York to a rural village in central New Jersey, cooperatively managing a women's coat and hat factory, as well as cooperatively run dairy, chicken, and crop farms. A school, factory, sewerage, and water plants would also be built.

Today the entire town of Roosevelt is listed on New Jersey's historic register and on the National Register of Historic Places.

Monmouth County's numerous shore communities would also become a large part of the Jewish vacation scene.

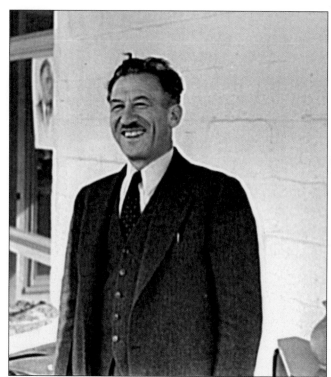

Benjamin Brown is known as the father of Jewish homesteaders. Brown was a Ukrainian American Jew who enjoyed great success in the livestock business and believed that a cooperative town was needed to both protect and propound Jewish values. During the Great Depression, he successfully lobbied the U.S. government to fund $500,000 for the new community.

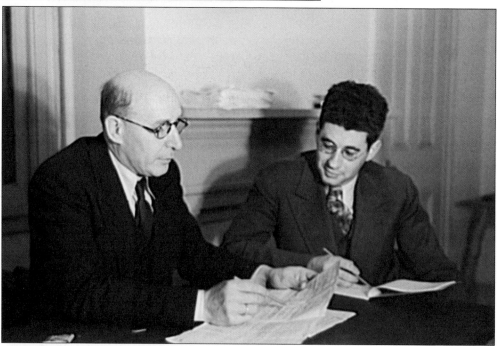

Samuel Finkler (left) and Harry Glanz are seen discussing applications from potential settlers. Finkler headed the government agency whose job was to select appropriate settlers to live in the new community. Some of the criteria that potential settlers had to meet included physical ability to succeed in a work atmosphere, mental toughness, and a degree of financial stability.

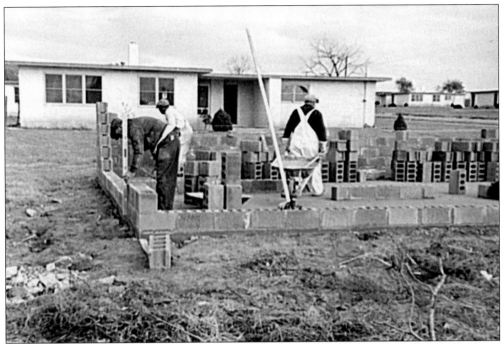

Construction of the first houses in the colony began in 1936. Each homeowner had to invest $500 toward the building effort. In all, 200 houses made up the original development plans.

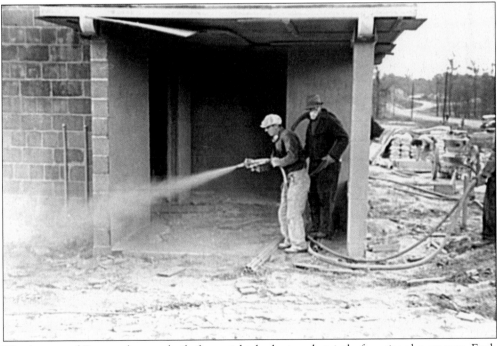

The houses of Roosevelt were built for a tight budget and strictly functional purposes. Each house received a simple coat of whitewash.

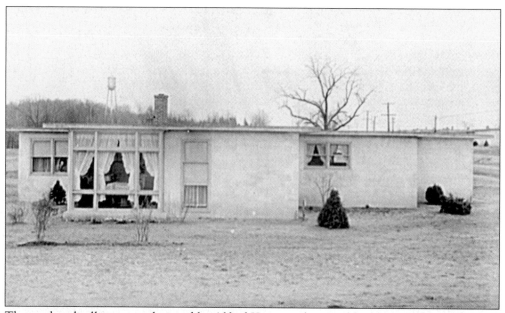

The modest dwellings were designed by Alfred Kastner who was, like many of the inhabitants, an immigrant from Europe.

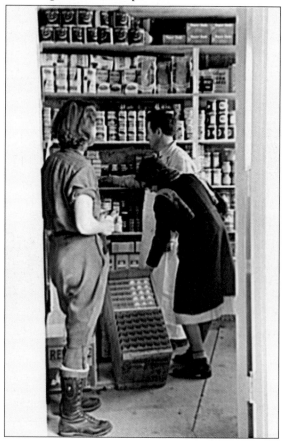

The first cooperative store that was owned by the community was operated by Natan Dubin. Dubin was one of the original Jersey homesteaders.

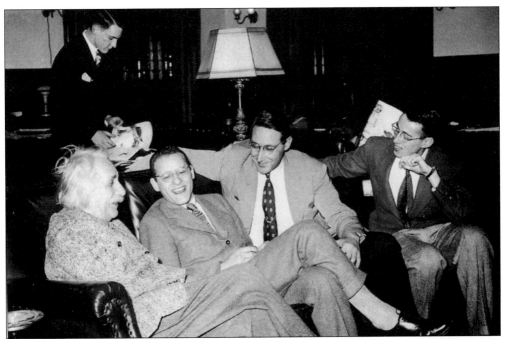

One of the main issues for opponents of the homesteads was the garment unions. During an era of financial uncertainty, the garment industry was loath to see an independent, nonunion shop open its doors. In this 1937 photograph taken in the offices of a garment factory in Hightstown, one sees the intervention of Albert Einstein, who was instrumental in pacifying the unions and paving the way for the homesteads to be approved.

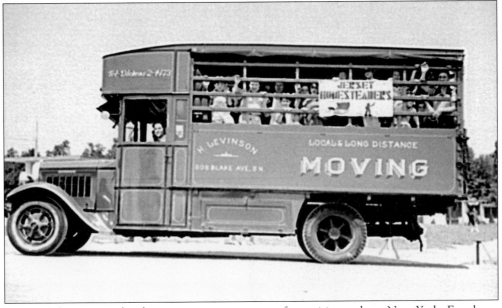

Many of the recruits for the new community came from cities such as New York. For them, moving to the homesteads was a homecoming of sorts, a reminder of the tightly knit villages of the Old World. Despite its caged appearance, the truck, and the employment that it represented, was a liberating sight during the Depression.

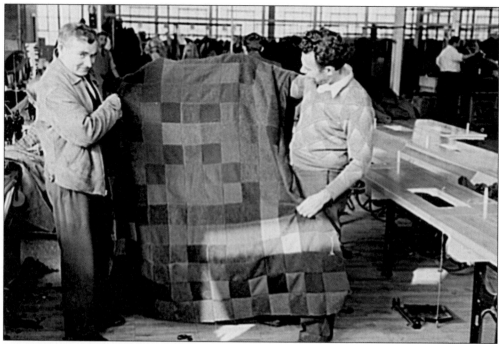

Harry Kaplan shows a blanket that he assembled out of scraps. The blanket, like the community that created it, was made of many diverse pieces coming from various backgrounds. A common Jewish identity and a desire to be independent united the town.

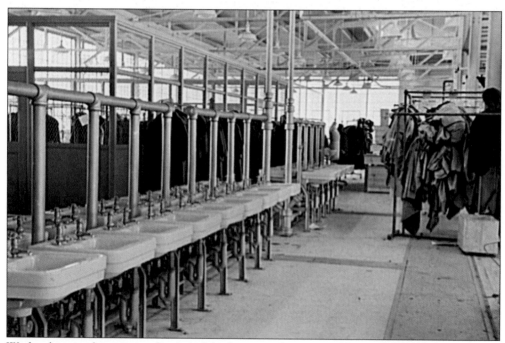

Washer bins in the garment factory of the homesteads were used by workers to clean up after a shift. These were one of the few "luxuries" provided to workers.

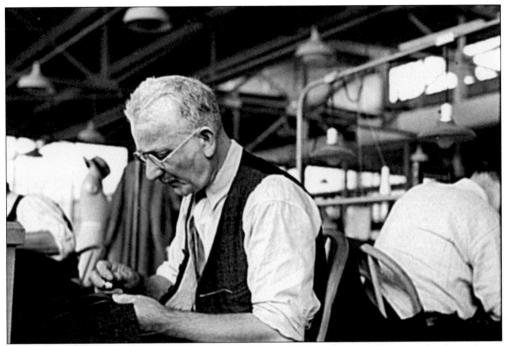

Although many of the founders had humble professions, such as working in the factories as Eugene Isaacs seen above and Philip Goldstien in the photograph below, their sons and daughters went on to become painters and professors, musicians and lawyers.

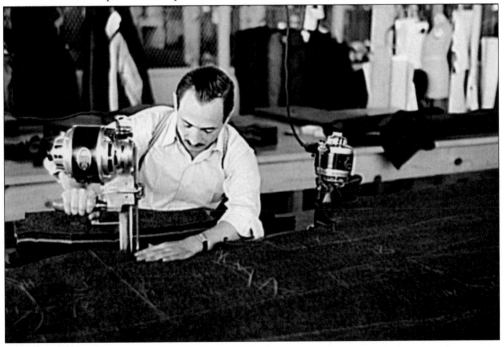

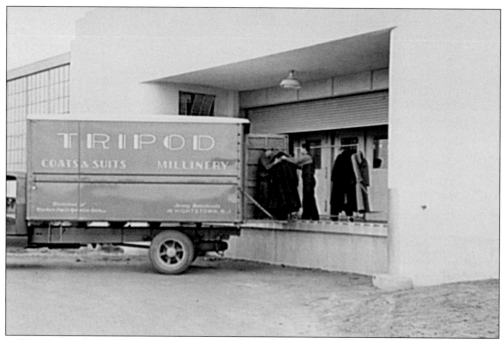

Following manufacturing, the garments would be shipped off in factory-owned trucks to retail stores in cities such as Philadelphia and New York City.

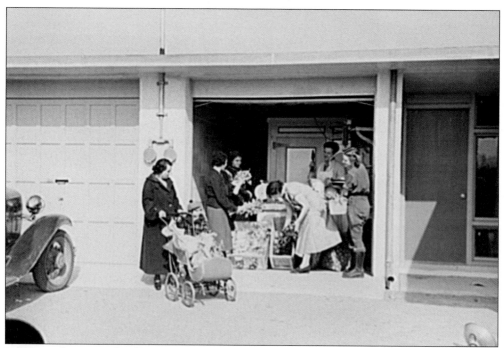

Jewish traditions and values were more than part of the town: they were the town. Many of the locals came from backgrounds of persecution, and they made sure to exercise their freedom of religion in their new home. Here homesteaders shop for meat in their own Kosher butcher shop.

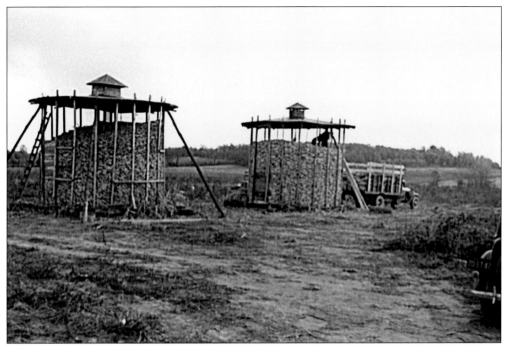

In this photograph, corn is being stored on the Hightstown farm. This would be used to feed the dairy cattle that would eventually become part of the Hightstown-Roosevelt community.

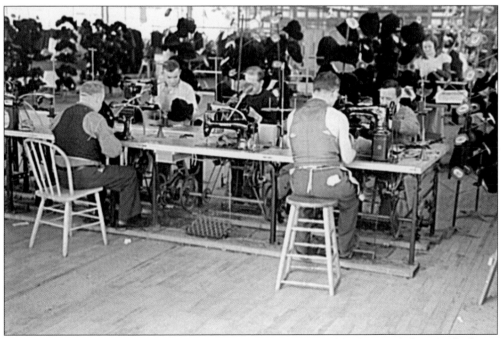

Many of the residents were skilled in the garment industry and had prior skills in such things as hat making.

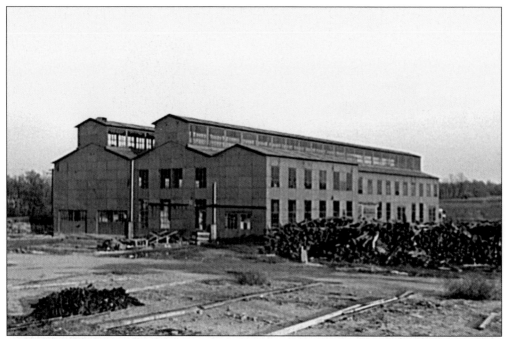

As the town grew, more business opportunities opened up for the residents, such as this new canning factory.

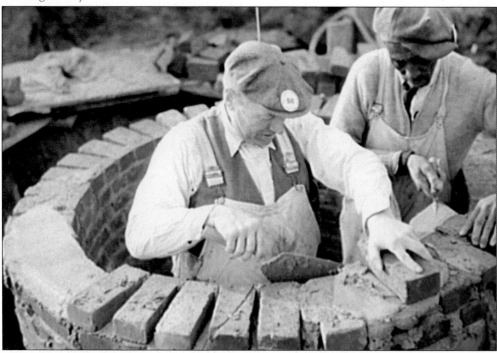

Old World trades found new use as the country worked its way through the Great Depression. Part of the stimulus for founding the community was to have self-sufficient workers available for work in their neighborhoods, such as the stone masons seen in this 1935 photograph of the homesteads being constructed in Hightstown.

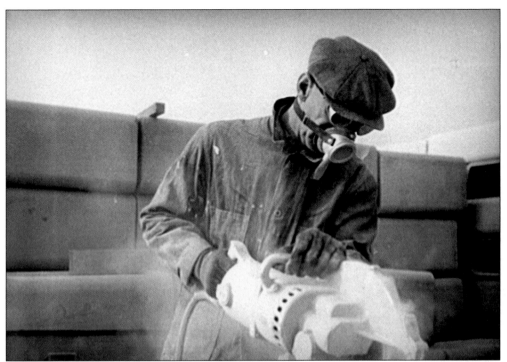

A tile worker sands tile at the construction site of Jersey Homesteads. The wearing of a protective mask by tradesmen was a relatively new concept at this time.

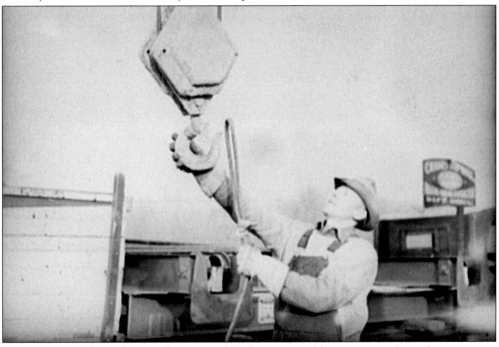

Jersey Homesteads was originally a part of Hightstown and became an independent entity in 1940. The attitude of many Hightstown inhabitants toward the homesteaders was often uneasy and suspicious as they watched the construction of a Jewish community in their backyard.

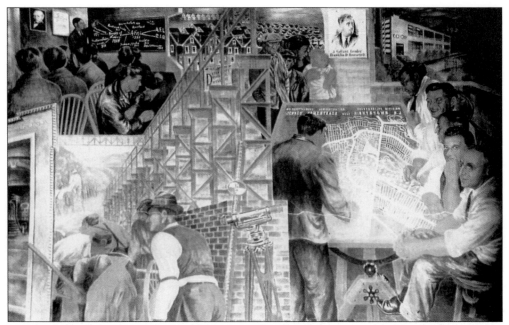

In this photograph is a mural painted on the wall of the elementary school by homestead artist Ben Shahn in the late 1930s. In this part of the mural Shahn shows the charting of the Jersey Homesteads at its inception. Note the prominence of the Franklin Delano Roosevelt portrait overlooking the planners. The town was renamed Roosevelt after the president's death.

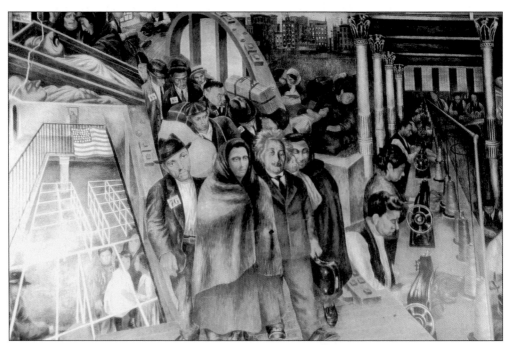

Visible in this section of the mural is Albert Einstein, as well as workers toiling at their sewing machines. Shahn went on to collaborate with Diego Rivera. He was also a court painter in several landmark cases in the United States.

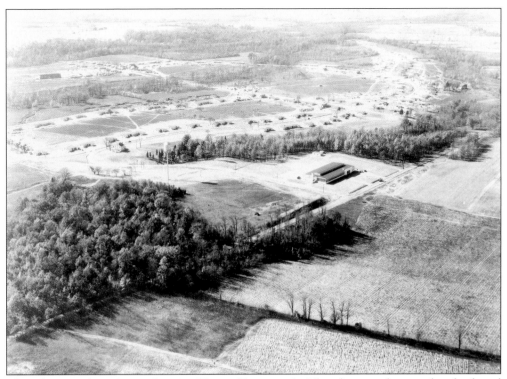

This photograph is an aerial view of Jersey Homesteads. The photograph was taken by famed photographer Dorothea Lange, who during the Depression years worked for the Federal Farm Administration documenting various government projects.

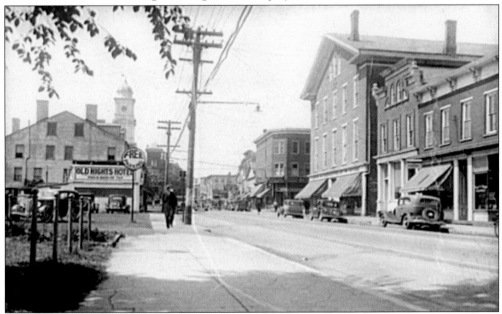

This early photograph is of downtown Hightstown. Jersey Homesteads' post office address and telephone exchange are permanently identified with Hightstown. Sold in 1940, the town incorporated as a separate township from Hightstown and became part of Monmouth County.

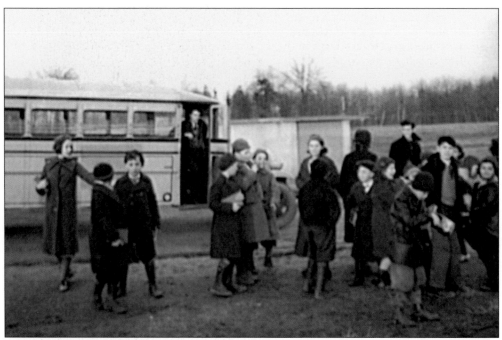

Roosevelt settlers were recruited through a network of Jewish newspapers and organizations, like the HIAS. Each family paid $500 to join the cooperative. They were by in large eastern European Jews, around 40, with one to five children ranging from grade to high school age. Most children were bused to nearby towns for their education.

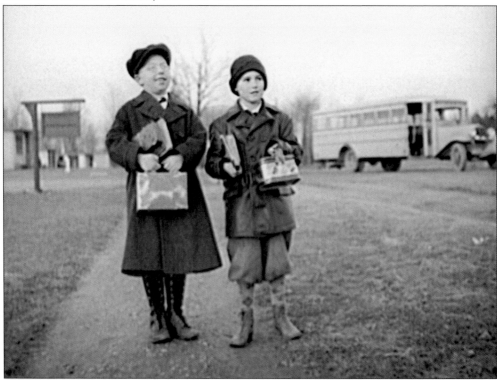

With the birth of their baby in October 1936, Mr. and Mrs. Philip Goldstein had the honor of claiming the first birth in the new colony of Jersey Homesteads.

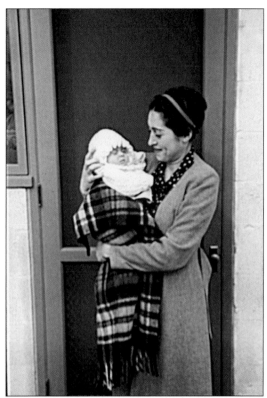

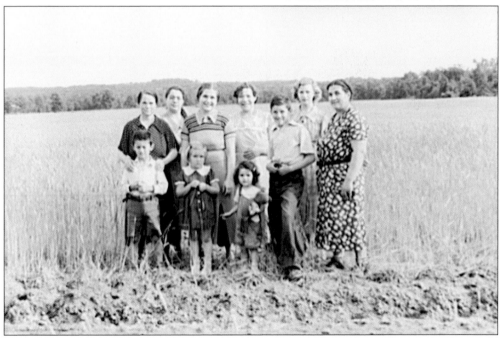

Even in this small community there was some controversy over who really was the first child born in Jersey Homesteads with the Cohens claiming that their daughter Frieda, seen as a two-year-old in this photograph, was the first birth in the colony.

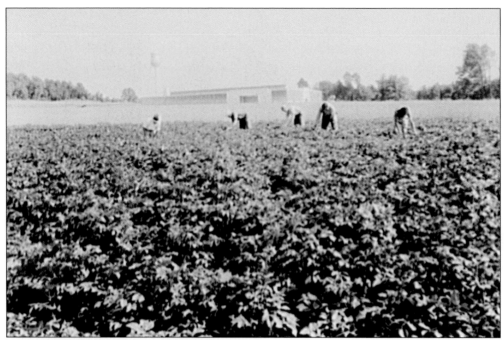

The Jersey Homesteads plan in Hightstown called for the resettlement of Jewish garment workers from New York to a rural village in central New Jersey. Here they would cooperatively, managing a women's coat and hat factory, as well as cooperatively run dairy, chicken, and crop farms such as the one in this image. Eventually 200 houses, a school, a factory, and sewage and water plants would be built.

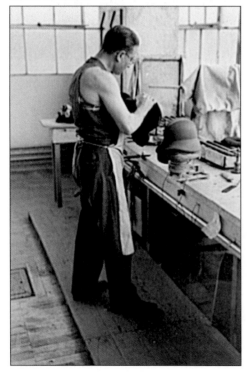

As World War II began, some manufacturers of ladies' clothing switched almost entirely to making military uniforms. Here a garment worker is making military uniforms.

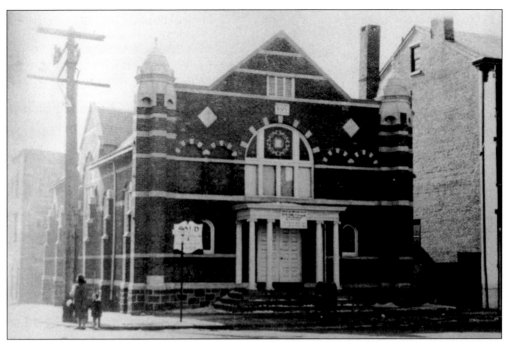

Trenton's organized Jewish roots began with the Har Sini Cemetery Association, which purchased a plot of land at Vroom and Liberty Streets for the city's first Jewish cemetery. This group would evolve into Trenton's first synagogue, Temple Har Sini, a Reform congregation. The congregation's first building was a former church on North Montgomery Street.

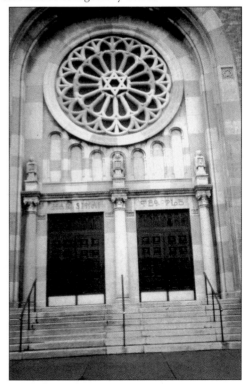

The present building, seen here, is located at 491 Bellevue Avenue and was built in 1929.

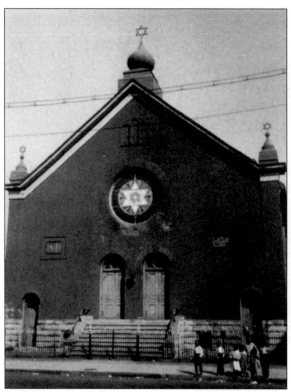

The earliest Orthodox congregation was Brothers of Israel, which was incorporated in 1883 and was lead by Rabbi Issachar Levin. By 1904, Congregation Brothers of Israel erected the city's first Talmud Torah, which was named after the father of Zionism, Dr. Theodor Herzl.

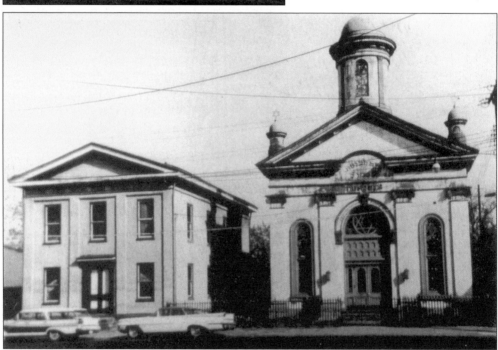

Organized in 1919, Congregation People of Truth (Anshei Emes) was located at 30–32 Union Street. This was another of the city's Orthodox congregations. The building to the left of the synagogue served as the Talmud Torah.

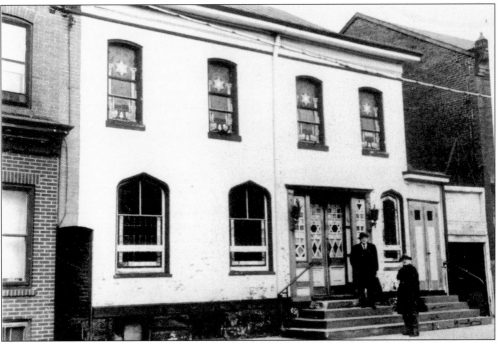

Congregation Anshei Fief was organized by former members who broke away from Congregation Anshei Emes. In the photograph, the building adjoining the synagogue is a *shodhet* or "ritual slaughter house."

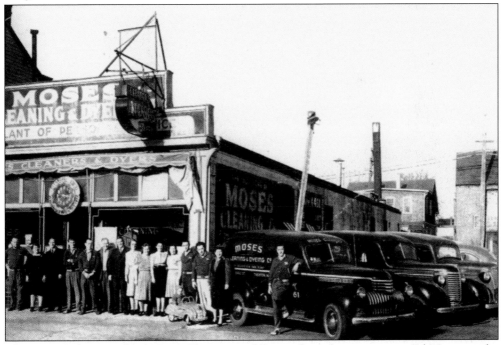

This c. 1935 photograph of Moses Cleaning and Dying shows business owner Ed Moses on the running board of one of his trucks. The store was one of the many that existed on South Broad Street in Trenton.

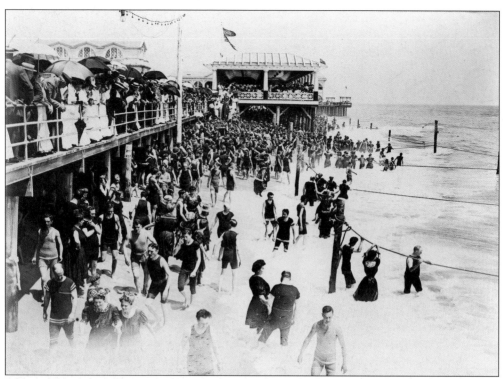

The term "down the shore" would become a common term among middle- and upper-middle-class Jews, and a favorite vacation spot was Asbury Park.

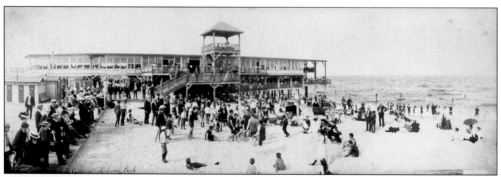

Bradley Beach, seen in this 1902 picture, was another popular Jersey Shore destination for South Jersey and Philadelphia Jews.

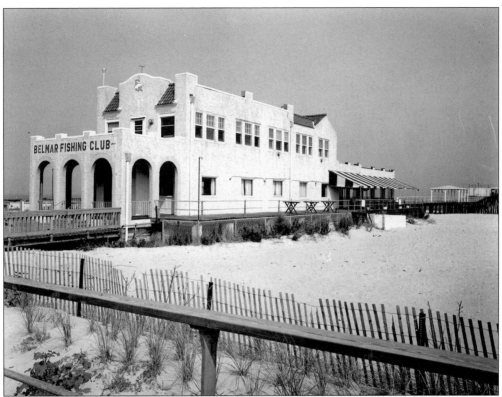

From the 1900s to the 1930s, Belmar was known as the place to live or vacation among the Jewish intelligentsia. Among the residents of the town was Yiddish writer Sholom Aleichem.

BAY VIEW HOUSE,

Centrally Located on the Water Front,

FIRST ESTABEISHED AND MOST POPUEAR FAMIEY HOUSE IN

Atlantic Highlands,   New Jersey.

NO HEBREWS TAKEN.

With clear anti-Semitism present in many of the hotels of the Jersey Shore region, Jews would soon establish their own hotels.

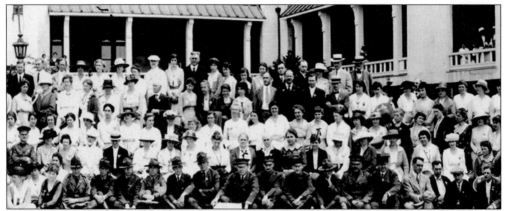

Opening day for the new Monterey Hotel in Asbury Park was June 25, 1919. Asbury Park and its grand hotels, like the Monterey, were the summer homes for many Jews from the urban areas of New Jersey.

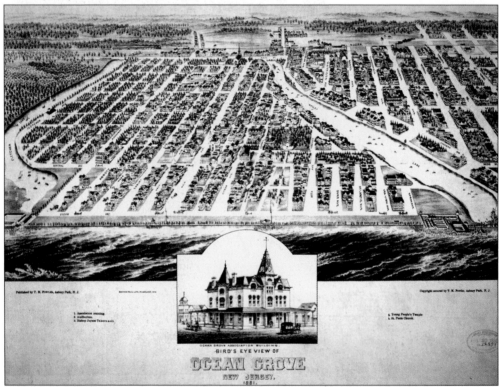

One of the strange quirks of the Jersey Shore was the fact that the very Jewish Asbury Park and Bradley Beaches bordered each side of the very Christian Ocean Grove Beach. The town started out as a Methodist camp meeting place, and the town's government was intertwined with the town's church leadership. Rules for the town included the requirement that males wear shirts while on the boardwalk, and likewise women had to cover their bathing suits while they strolled the boardwalk. The township managed to ban automobiles from its streets every Sunday until a court decision in 1979 declared the law unconstitutional. Although there were no signs saying No Jews Allowed, for many years it was a known fact that Jews, as well as African Americans, were not welcome in the community of Ocean Grove.

Congregation Brothers of Israel was organized in 1898. Started by seven immigrant families who had arrived in Long Beach as part of the second wave of immigration from Russia and Poland, Brothers of Israel would grow to become the largest Orthodox synagogue in the region.

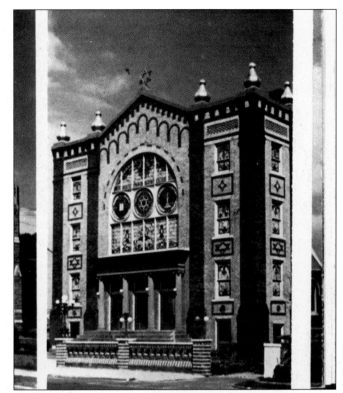

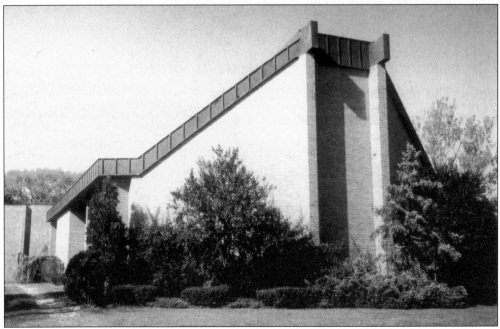

Today a large Syrian Sephardic population resides in Deal. Founded in 1940, the Synagogue of Deal has grown over the years as the population of vacationers eventually became full-time residents of the community. In addition to the new synagogue, the community has built a Yeshiva day and high school, a mikvah, and senior citizen housing.

ACROSS AMERICA, PEOPLE ARE DISCOVERING SOMETHING WONDERFUL. *THEIR HERITAGE.*

Arcadia Publishing is the leading local history publisher in the United States. With more than 3,000 titles in print and hundreds of new titles released every year, Arcadia has extensive specialized experience chronicling the history of communities and celebrating America's hidden stories, bringing to life the people, places, and events from the past. To discover the history of other communities across the nation, please visit:

www.arcadiapublishing.com

Customized search tools allow you to find regional history books about the town where you grew up, the cities where your friends and family live, the town where your parents met, or even that retirement spot you've been dreaming about.

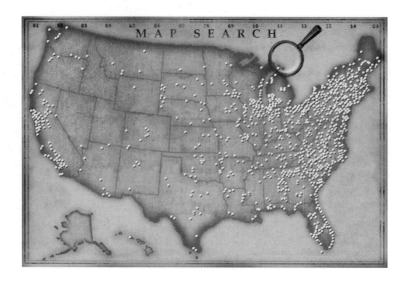